Christians at the Crossroads

PATRICIA HIGTON

Christians at the Crossroads

Revival and Judgement —
A Prophetic Challenge

MarshallPickering
An Imprint of HarperCollinsPublishers

First published in Great Britain in 1991 by
Marshall Pickering

Marshall Pickering is an imprint of
HarperCollins Religious Division,
part of the HarperCollins Publishing Group
77–85 Fulham Palace Road,
London W6 8JB

Printed and bound in Great Britain by
HarperCollinsManufacturing, Glasgow
Glasgow

Contents

Dedication

To Tony: my husband, friend and partner in the Gospel

Acknowledgements

I am grateful to Christine Whitell, the Publishing Manager, for encouraging me to write this book, when it had never occurred to me that I could do such a thing; to Tony for carefully reading it through before it went to the typist, for the use of some of his research on interfaith matters in Chapter 5 and for his encouragement throughout. Also to Sally Robinson who developed a unique gift for deciphering my illegible scrawl, spending weeks transferring it to the word processor; and to Sonia Lightfoot and her faithful prayer group.

Finally I am grateful to the Body of Christ in Hawkwell Parish, especially to the leaders, for recognising that I need ''space'' to develop the ministry to which they believe God has called me.

Patricia Higton

Introduction

I believe we are facing the biggest crisis in the Church in the West since the Reformation, if not since the Church began. In the near future, perhaps by the end of the millennium, every Christian, every local church, every denomination will face a significant testing time. Some who appeared to be true believers will turn back from the Christian faith. Others will turn to the left or to the right. This is the broad road, the easy path, the way of compromise or deceit. Too late they will realise they are part of a Church which is no church. Some, by the grace of God, will forge ahead along the difficult road, the way of the Cross.

What is the decision which Christians at least in the West or Westernized nations, will be called upon to make? It is whether we will persevere in wholehearted belief in the Jesus Christ of revelation rather than imagination. Will we then go on to proclaim him in the redeeming power of his death and resurrection, as the ONLY way of salvation?

Most believers in the evangelical and/or renewal scene, as well as many in other traditions, could never imagine giving in to temptation to believe anything else. It is important therefore to understand just how subtle and powerful the temptation to compromise will be.

We shall examine the deceit of the New Age and later

the interfaith movement. The reasons why many might succumb will be found not just in the subtlety of these temptations, but in the weaknesses in the evangelical and renewal circles in which many of us move. We shall look at a broad canvas of God's dealings with nations, showing how dangerous the situation is for the Church in the West. Could we even be in the Last Days? What is God's true purpose for his Church in the midst of all these events?

If by the grace and power of God, we overcome, what is the way ahead for Christians in the last decade of this millennium? But first, and interwoven throughout the book, we shall consider what we are to make of the current euphoria about revival, whilst others issue dire warnings about judgement.

CHAPTER ONE

Revival or Judgement?

Disasters come and disasters go. Some are remembered only by those involved – the injured, bereaved, those who went to the rescue. Others make a major impact on an area, a nation or the world, and will be remembered for at least decades to come. There were many such towards the end of the last decade. Chernobyl was one which may well have changed the course of history. In our own country, names such as Zeebrugge, Hungerford and Lockerbie are amongst many which immediately conjure up pictures of horrifying tragedies.

News of one such disaster was filtering through on the radio as I was getting ready to lead a Faith-Sharing Evening for a church in the Midlands. The church had been preparing in prayer and practical ways. The team were nervous – a "first" for most of them. The idea was simple enough. Church members had invited friends and neighbours on an "each-one-bring-one" basis. We all enjoyed a meal together, then the team acted out a role-play, which had its lighter moments but centred on a presentation of the Gospel. My part included asking the audience, as they sat at their tables, just two questions. Everyone jotted down an answer which was only for the eyes of the individual concerned. The idea was to get people thinking about eternal issues in an informal atmosphere. I asked everyone present

1

whether, if they were to die suddenly, that night, they thought they would go to heaven, and if so why they thought God might welcome them. Some will recognise the questions as similar to those integral to the "Evangelism Explosion" method of witnessing training, although the Faith-Sharing suppers were our own idea.

Usually I would bring in humour at that point to put people at their ease, but that particular evening, it was impossible to be light-hearted. There had been subdued conversation around the meal tables about the news on the radio that afternoon. One man in our audience had actually been at the scene, cheering on the Nottingham Forest side at the Hillsborough football stadium. Gradually, the fans dimly perceived that something was sadly amiss on the other side. Their cheers faded away as they were urged by the police over the loud speakers to disperse quietly. By the evening it was clear that a tragedy had occurred with terrible loss of life, but details were still scarce. Two policemen had also joined us for the meal – they could identify with what their colleagues were going through.

The evening drew to a close. The Gospel had been explained in a non-threatening but powerful way. You could have heard a pin drop. As the cups of coffee were served, everyone had a card to fill in with at least their name and address, but with an invitation to indicate more than that. Some might want to join a "Christianity Explained" group. Others might even want to indicate that they had taken the step of putting their faith in Jesus Christ, at the point when I had led in a prayer of commitment. In the only other similar Faith-Sharing Evening which I had led, two or three people had responded in this way.

2

We collected the cards and went back to the Vicarage. We were longing to look at the cards, but we wanted to hear the news too. We switched on the television. What a mixture of emotions we experienced that night! Tears pricked our eyes as the senseless tragedy unfolded on the screen. This time there had been no hooliganism – just mistakes and meaninglessness. Liverpool supporters, helpless to escape, were crushed to death as wave after wave of other Liverpool fans, equally helpless to retreat, flooded into that section of the stadium, overcrowding it far beyond the point of human ability to survive. Young and old, but mainly young, dying in agony, or horribly injured. Because of the crowd control barriers, there was no way out. Ten, twenty, thirty . . . . the death count rose . . . . seventy, eighty, ninety.

We counted the cards. There weren't just names and addresses. There were ticks on card after card, many indicating they had made a commitment to Christ and/or wanted to join the discipleship class. One, two, three . . . . seventeen, eighteen, nineteen. Tears of joy. More than a quarter of those there. By the close of the morning service the next day, twenty-two people had taken a definite step forward along the road of faith in Jesus. That same weekend well over ninety people had died and two hundred had been injured in a football stadium not so far away, in the worst British football disaster in history.

For a brief time, the issues of life, death and eternity were very real. A significant but tragic factor in a weekend which, if followed up wisely, may have been a turning point for an average Anglican church, not at all used to evangelistic events.

That combination of circumstances helped me to understand why I react with grief as well as joy when Christians talk about not tens, but thousands turning to God in revival. I remember one occasion when I was sitting on the platform at a Spring Harvest Celebration. "Spring Harvest" – that major annual Christian event in the U.K. Sixty to seventy thousand people staying for a week at a time in holiday camps in a number of locations over a three- or four-week period, making their selection from the wide range on offer of seminars, workshops, talkbacks, celebrations, youth activities. Evangelical in its basis with an openness to renewal, it attracts Christians from a wide variety of church backgrounds.

The speaker on that Good Friday morning was the well-known evangelist, Luis Palau. When he had been introduced to the other speakers earlier, we had been impressed by the warmth of his personality. Now he spoke with profound simplicity on the efficacy of the cross of Christ for salvation and the victorious Christian life. One could sense the rapport with the two thousand (mainly young) attentive listeners. He was moved to say in his attractive Argentinian accent: "I sense that revival is coming and as I look at you young people and watch the way you worship, I believe I can say that revival is already here."

Why did I sense such a sinking feeling in my spirit? After all, had I not longed for revival since I was a teenager? I had never had any problem with the supernatural side of Christianity. (What other side should there be?) As a young child I had known when God committed himself to me and I to him for eternity. The ability for spiritual understanding in a child should

4

never be under-estimated. I knew when I was seven that the death of Christ was the way to an eternal relationship with my Father as I put my trust in him.

I knew that God could break through the ordinary and mundane. He often did in my young life. The material world to me was just an environment which happened to be a present context for true reality. Even as a teenager, what was going on in my spirit was far more important to me. When I had an opportunity to be involved in my first evangelistic mission, I expected God to work in power. I remember chatting about Christianity to a teenager who was an avowed atheist. As I dealt, rather inadequately, with her questions on creation and evolution, and I spoke about the Son of God being involved in creation, the Son who then died for her, I saw the girl change before my eyes. The light dawned, and she became a Christian in a moment of time. She wrote to me years later to say that she had never looked back from that day. I knew therefore what the Holy Spirit could do – in fact I had to learn rather painfully that he could work in the lives of men and women in more gradual and seemingly ordinary ways. I had to learn even more painfully to get involved in the mundane side of life, and am still learning to trust over the smaller details.

When I first read books about revival, to me that was just the obvious next step in God's dealing with his people. He is sovereign, he is almighty, he intervenes in the lives of his created ones and he intervenes in history. A God who could or would not do this was evidently not the God of the Bible nor the God I knew. The emasculated God of liberal theology held no appeal for me, except, interestingly enough, when I went through a major period of doubt in my early twenties. I realised that in the mystery of his purposes there are long periods of time when it seems God is silent, for I had experienced times of darkness in my personal life. Long ago Israel had experienced four centuries of the silence of God before Christ came. But revival would come and I was convinced it would be in my country in my lifetime.

I had an almost intuitive awareness of what it would be like to be caught up in a revival. This was before I ever read of the Hebrides' revival in the 1950s, the Welsh revival at the beginning of the century, the Moody/Sankey revival a few decades earlier, the Wesleyan revival of the eighteenth century, or the more recent revivals in other parts of the world up to the present day.

I knew when Renewal came, that it was not revival, even though some claimed otherwise. For, although hundreds of thousands of Christians throughout the world from the 1960s onwards have experienced a greater release of God's power, manifested especially in worship and the gifts of the Spirit, the world remains largely untouched. The Charismatic Movement also seems to do little to help deepen the holiness of God's people. I believe that true revival will bring the children of God into such an awareness of his holiness that we shall not be able to rest until we know what it is to take up the cross. The effect of this on individual Christians, a local church, even whole sections of the wider Church, will lead to such a release of the power of God that unbelievers will be drawn by the Holy Spirit into the presence of God. The lives of tens, hundreds, even thousands, could be transformed in a sovereign way.

When my husband, Tony, and I first took out teams from our church to other churches, this was our message. Tony sometimes preached on the five "R's": Repentance, Renewal, Restoration, Revival and Return.

Repentance

We spoke of the initial step of salvation and how a profession of faith which does not include repentance leads at best to a crippled Christian life. This is the penalty for the preaching of a Gospel which stresses only the benefits of turning to Christ, leading to a self-centred Christianity which is a contradiction in terms. The remedy can only be belated repentance.

Renewal

We encouraged people to seek the baptism in the Spirit. Tony and I had become convinced in the 1960s that John the Baptist's dual description of Jesus' role as "the Lamb of God who takes away the sin of the world" *and* "he who will baptise with the Holy Spirit" (John 1:29,33) was meant to be the experience of every believer. The lives of the early Christians were evidently characterised by power. What a contrast to the lives of most Christians in the mid 1960s. Although I personally was very much aware of the power of God I was a very poor channel of that power. Yes, the power was there as in every believer, for "if anyone does not have the Spirit of Christ, he does not belong to Christ" (Romans 8:9). But I needed to humble myself to ask in prayer for a release of that power. As godly men prayed for me in a vicarage in Gillingham in 1967, after what seemed an age when nothing happened, the study was suddenly transformed as if into Calvary, and I was kneeling at the foot of the cross. The realisation flooded my being that Jesus had died not only for my forgiveness and to open the way to heaven, but to fill me with power to serve him. I spoke in a heavenly language words of pure praise, and was able to go back to witness to staff and students in the school where I taught. Other gifts of the Spirit followed later, a process not without pain.

Restoration

As for restoration, we meant by that, not a triumphalist view of eschatology, but rather the need for the Church to be restored to biblical principles in the power of the Spirit. God was soon to lead us into a dual ministry of speaking out against glaring unbiblical teaching, and encouraging churches in a flexible, practical programme to help them to become united on a biblical basis, in order to be effective in every-member ministry, intercession and evangelism.

Revival

Before we spoke on the final point of the possible imminent return of our Lord, we encouraged congregations to pray for revival. To whet their appetites we would perhaps tell them about the Hebrides' revival in the 1950s. On the island of Lewis seven men and two elderly women covenanted to pray, that they would give God no rest until the Church brought more glory to him on earth. They were deeply concerned about moral decline and young people leaving the Church. They prayed three nights a week for months. Then one night a young man read from Psalm 24: "Who shall ascend into the hill of the Lord? or who shall stand in his holy place? He that hath clean hands, and a pure heart . . . He shall receive the blessing from the Lord" (A.V.). He paused, then said to the others "Brethren, isn't it so much humbug to be waiting on God night after night, if we ourselves are not right with him? Is my heart pure? Are my hands clean?" The Rev. Duncan Campbell, whom God used as a key person later in the revival, wrote, "God swept the meeting, and seven men were now lying prostrate before him. At the other end of the parish the two elderly sisters were lying prostrate in their cottage – not in bed,for how could they sleep with so many souls perishing? That same morning, one sister (Peggy) saw in a God-given vision, hundreds being swept into the Kingdom, the churches crowded, and the Lamb in the midst of the throne with the keys of heaven in his hand."

Peggy was told by God that a man called Duncan Campbell would be used, so a message was sent to him. He had been booked to speak elsewhere, but only a fortnight before he received the message, events had brought about a cancellation, which enabled him to accept the invitation to Lewis. On arrival he went to preach in the kirk. Nothing much happened and he closed the service. The young man mentioned earlier cried out in his disappointment, "O God, you promised!" The people began to return and fill the church. Campbell preached again and God's power fell. People cried out in all parts of the church for God to save them. Duncan dismissed the congregation, but had to preach to a crowd which gathered in another part of the village in the early hours.

In the village of Arnol in Lewis, there was no response in the first few meetings, so a prayer meeting was held at night. The members sensed God had answered. On leaving the cottage they found the villagers leaving their cottages and making their way to a point in the village, as if drawn by some unseen force. Duncan preached and revival broke out.

In these ways we encouraged people to believe that God can do it again, but on a bigger scale, in the U.K., and perhaps generally in the West and Westernised nations. We explained that Christianity is spreading in an amazing way in other parts of the world such as South Korea, other parts of the Far East, including China; parts of Africa and South America. Although the Church has been declining in the West, we pointed to encouraging signs, particularly the rapid spread of prayer groups through organisations such as Lydia and Intercessors for Britain.

Surely, we should have rejoiced when the cry, "Revival is coming" began to be voiced a few years later by Christian leaders in renewal circles throughout the country. It wasn't as if Christians were expecting God to work whilst they slept. Not only was there more prayer, but people worked hard for the Billy Graham crusades and the results were encouraging. Churches, including the so-called "house churches", became more outward looking, and it was not long before the 1990s were declared by denominations across the board, and even worldwide, as the Decade of Evangelism.

The phenomenon of Praise Marches caught on. Some of us had long ago discovered that a useful preliminary to evangelism in an area, was for a group of Christians, perhaps housegroup members, to engage in prayer walks. Instead of just praying for unbelievers at home, it was good to walk the streets, discreetly praying for the homes as the Holy Spirit led. Jesus' victory was declared over the powers of darkness and so battle was joined! But Graham Kendrick, with his "Make Way" music, gave us a tool to do this more publicly and effectively. Soon everyone, it seemed, was getting involved, with the highlight at the end of the 1980s of a quarter of a million Christians taking to the streets, making a joyful noise. Sadly, it went almost unnoticed by the press, who would have been much more interested if a mob had gone on the rampage. They had obviously failed to see that Christians were on the warpath against the real enemy.

Why then my unfortunate negative reaction when Luis Palau made that remark at Spring Harvest about revival coming? Was it just that, as in the springtime of Charistmatic Renewal I had known that that was not revival, so I knew that, however uplifting the worship at Spring Harvest, and however eager the young people, that too was not revival?

Was it because of what happened when I was one of a crowd of ten thousand at a John Wimber rally? I was right at the back of the gallery with a good view of most of the auditorium. I had read two of Wimber's books, and thought I agreed with much of his teaching. I had never been free to go to one of his seminars on signs and wonders, but had heard good, even amazing, reports from those who had. It seemed that this man had a

11

Spirit-anointed ministry, particularly in the exercise of "the word of knowledge". Wonderfully used to encourage others to operate in the realm of the supernatural, this ministry was attested by signs following, especially in deliverance and healing. Some, initially untouched by renewal, now took their first steps in walking on the water. It was known as the Third Wave (the first being Pentecostalism, the second Renewal), and thousands of Christians were swept along by this tide. I went to the rally to learn as much as possible. I can only say that I was devastated by the atmosphere.

The audience was in high spirits. Nothing wrong with that, especially as for many it was the last meeting of a conference. But the sign-seekers were there in their hundreds, craning their necks for the latest miracle. A coach-load in front of me had got the shakes. They were obviously determined to shake throughout the whole rally, to prove to the rest of us that they had "the anointing". There were the screamers too. All the time I was trying to remind myself of two things. One was that when revival comes there are bound to be strange manifestations which will put off some. This was the case in Wesley's day and has been in most revivals. Secondly I was aware that some who long earnestly for revival might react against it when it comes, especially those who have not kept in step with the Spirit. Leaders in particular can be open to God at one time, but sadly close up later, especially if others are used to spearhead a new work of God. In view of this, I was trying to ensure that my attitude was one of openness and willingness to learn, whilst guarding against gullibility on the one hand and a tendency to a cynical sense of humour on the other. But when the speaker on the platform said, ''Everything you see happening around you is of the Holy Spirit'', I cringed. No doubt some of it was, but there was so much that was obviously fleshly and some things that might have fallen into a worse category. A Christian friend of ours who had once been deeply involved in the occult, said that before he was converted he would have ensured he attended any similar meeting in his area for his own dark purposes. There was no safeguard against such an awful possibility when people in the meeting were encouraged to pray for one another for healing. When we visited the refreshment booths outside in the break, it was every man for himself, the atmosphere indistinguishable from that at a secular show. I have no doubt that other Wimber meetings were totally different, but the congregation at that particular one was so lacking in reverence that it could only have been in the overruling mercy of God if people were touched by his power that day.

No, my reaction against statements about revival was not because of any confusion by some people of recent movements such as Charismatic Renewal, or wonderful times of worship at Spring Harvest, or the Third Wave, with revival. Nor was it that so much that has been of God in the last twenty-five years has failed to result in deeper holiness. In any case, I believe that is now changing. In one of the last issues of *Renewal* magazine in the 1980s, a number of church leaders wrote articles on the subject of revival, and several mentioned the need for deeper holiness. John Wimber announced his intention to hold seminars on the subject, acknowledging that the order in his life had been to experience God's power first, before his holiness. In many ways

13

that makes sense, because gifts can be given and used immediately whereas fruit takes time to grow. The very experience of being used as instruments of God's power, knowing it is all of him and none of us, can throw us back on his resources. Gradually a longing builds up to be purer channels for his service. Unfortunately, the opposite can also be true, when people become proud in the use of the gifts and try to rob God of the glory.

There is no doubt that a real hunger and thirst for righteousness is beginning to develop in whole sections of the Body of Christ in this country. In our own church there was a new atmosphere at the beginning of 1990. It was not something we could have laid on for the beginning of a new decade. We had a Central Meeting for all our housegroups in the second week of the New Year. We had planned the evening carefully, but the Holy Spirit swept our plans away. There was a sense of the majesty of God and of our unworthiness. Prayers, prophecies and other gifts followed one after the other, all on the theme of telling God that we wanted to be more like him, but did not know where to start. In the past we had tried to pray for revival, but did not know how. We had also experienced times when we had knelt spontaneously as a congregation in the awesome presence of God. But somehow in the silence that followed during that evening, we just knew that God had taken us in hand as a people, and he was going to show us step by step. All sense of striving had gone, we knew the process of revival had begun in a tiny way. It was a cloud as small as a man's hand, but the rains would follow. In some churches we have visited up and down the country, God is doing the same thing.

But the reaction I had of both grief and joy at the mention of revival in that Spring Harvest meeting, remains. God has begun, in a tiny way, to revive his Church in the West and Westernised nations. *If* he continues to show mercy and we continue in obedience and faith, the process will continue. But this is no time for euphoria. I "saw" with my spiritual sight in a prayer meeting for this country, an impression of Jesus pointing his sword of judgement at the heart of this nation. That was a few years ago, and I have never seen the sword lifted. At the point of his sword is the Church itself, "for it is time for judgement to begin with the family of God; and if it begins with us, what will the outcome be for those who do not obey the Gospel of God?" (1 Peter 4:17).

Revival and Judgement

There are those Christian leaders who stress revival and others who stress judgement. Who is right? When people have asked us, we have sometimes given the answer: "Both." Doubtless few would disagree with that, whatever their own emphasis. But in the last year I have come to see some of the reasons why the revival which is to come could be the most difficult time ever experienced by the Church of God since its early years.

I believe it will be a time rather like that experienced by St John when offered the little scroll by the angel, as described in Revelation chapter 10. In verse 10 we read that John took the scroll and ate it. "It tasted sweet as honey in my mouth, but when I had eaten it my stomach turned sour." Then John was commanded to prophesy further about nations and kings. His prophecies were to reveal both the wonder of heaven and terror on earth.

So I believe it will be for God's people in the days to come. We shall taste what he offers to us in revival and it will bring us great joy. But as revival takes effect we shall experience grief as we see some of the results of it. Revival this time will be born out of judgement and result in further judgement. In the past each revival has had its own characteristics. For example, the revival in Ruanda this century featured open confession of sin amongst groups of believers. Every revival, however, has inevitably included judgement to some extent, as there are those who react against what God is doing. But judgement will be the *main* characteristic this time.

For the Church, as God leads us into holiness, the process of purification will be the crucible from which revival emerges. This will be difficult for all of us. For too long there has been glory without the cross in many renewal circles. Second generation "charismatics" have usually not had to face the same opposition as those who were amongst the first to pave the way. Greater freedom in worship is generally accepted in many Christian circles, some of which would not own the renewal label. Where there is tension over these matters, as is still often the case at local church level in the historic denominations, there is usually an area celebration to encourage the faith of those wanting greater freedom. Renewal has been through various phases – the rather intense worship of the "Fisher Folk" phase, the emphasis on community, the proclamation type of worship, the signs and wonders phase. Always, always an emphasis on healing and counselling. The house churches contributed their triumphalistic approach, seeking to usher in the rule of Christ here and now. The evangelicals were rediscovering our responsibility to society. Then came the outward-looking phase. It all began to come together in a healthy desire at least to try to work together, charismatic and "non-charismatic", high church, low church, any denomination or none, in the decade of evangelism. Even where there is no co-operation, the aim is the same – to reach the whole world with the Gospel and win as many as possible to Christ by the end of the second millennium. No sooner were plans under way, than Eastern Europe suddenly threw off its shackles and a huge door, hitherto shut and bolted, opened wide. All heady stuff. Yet I have just received through the post a mailing from a well-established renewal organisation rejoicing in amazing developments in the world and church scene, but not a single note of warning of danger to come.

It is in order to prepare us, as well as to make us more like him, that Jesus will lead his people through a purifying process. A preparation for a time of severe testing as to whether those who call themselves Christians are going to hold to the belief that Jesus is the *only* way. "For there is no other name under heaven given to men by which we must be saved" (Acts 4:12). Those Christians living in countries which have recently been, or are now, in the throes of persecution will be far better prepared. The testing time will be far more severe for those in the Church in the West or Westernised nations.

As the true, more purified Church emerges, so the revival will begin to have major impact on the world. But I do not believe at this stage we shall be seeing societies and nations transformed. We should always work for that, of course, because Christians should be in the forefront of campaigning for freedom, justice, the sanctity of human life etc., and no doubt there will be some victories. But the main result of the revival will be to rescue many from the clutches of the enemy, for "night is coming, when no one can work" (John 9:4).

Just as the revival for the Church will be born in the judgement of purification and result in the judgement of separation between true and false, so judgement will be a feature for the unbeliever. It is because of this aspect, for believer and unbeliever alike, that I reacted as I did when Luis Palau spoke of revival, and when other Christian leaders predict that revival is round the corner for the West.

God spoke to our own nation by answering our prayers during World War II, giving us not only victory but a large measure of prosperity. It is no coincidence that the first Billy Graham crusade in London was able to take place at a time when we were emerging from postwar austerity. It was a time of transition. Our Queen had been crowned, Everest conquered, cities rebuilt. Would we honour the many vows made to almighty God during the terrible war years? A minority responded in faith, but the majority went their own way, the way of materialism, hedonism (living for pleasure), faster and faster down the slippery slope of decadence.

The main way left to God to speak now is through redemptive judgement. But how will he judge? No one (except, apparently liberal theologians) can rule out "acts of God", direct intervention, but the main form of judgement will always be the way which is obvious in

18

its justice: the consequences inherent in our chosen course of action. The gales in October 1987 which destroyed fifteen million trees, were followed by similar storms in January 1990 in the South of England and Europe, leaving a trail of havoc, including deaths and injuries. Normally such gales have only happened once every two hundred years. It is possible they were just a small part of the evidence of the greenhouse effect brought about by our unthinking use of the resources of planet Earth. As is so often the case, an article in a secular newspaper was more perceptive than comments from most pulpits. Paul Johnson wrote in the *Daily Mail* on 27th January 1990: ''I am willing to bet that a great many people who do not normally think of God at all, found themselves saying a silent prayer on Thursday – a prayer for protection against the elements, and perhaps too, a prayer of relief and gratitude when the wind died down, and they realised that they . . . were safe. They may not go to church tomorrow in consequence. But, all the same, when the great wind came, it was a sobering moment, a thought-provoking moment, a moment when they, and all of us, realised that this rich, complicated, urban, electronic, computerised world we have created, is a very fragile thing in the face of aroused Nature, and that we clever, cosseted humans are vulnerable creatures, who can be tossed into eternity without warning.''

As the light of a purified Church shines brighter, so many will be rescued from the increasing darkness of a society under judgement. But the result will be further judgement on those who do not respond. They will be confirmed in their own choice of a way diametrically opposed to the way of the Cross. The West and eventually the world will enter what they think is a New Age, only to find it is the darkest of Dark Ages.

I hope that, even though aware of all this, we shall still pray for revival. Judgement will come relentlessly, but revival will ensure the rescue of as many as possible. Besides, in the midst of the momentous events to come, there will be times of great joy and power, far exceeding anything experienced by the Church in the last thirty years. For it will be the joy of the Cross, not unthinking euphoria.

A member of the Evangelical Sisterhood of Mary in Darmstadt, West Germany, had a "picture" in prayer of a coachload of Christians. They were singing and praising, oblivious of the dangers as their coach hurtled along a narrow, winding, mountainous road, the darkness of a steep ravine only inches away, ready to engulf them.

As we pray, praise and march for revival, let us do it in awareness to some extent at least, of the nature of the God we serve, and the way he works. Moses, Miriam and the Israelites sang to the Lord: "Who among the gods is like you, O Lord? Who is like you – majestic in holiness, awesome in glory, working wonders?" (Exodus 15:11). As we sing the modern version of those words, do we remember the context? The Israelites had just come through the Red Sea, narrowly escaping the Egyptians, after a terrible time of plague after plague, the first few of which had afflicted the people of God as well as of Egypt.

David later encouraged the people in a psalm of praise:

"Give thanks to the Lord, call on his name,
make known among the nations what he has done.
Sing to him, sing praise to him;
tell of all his wonderful acts.
Glory in his holy name;
let the hearts of those who seek the Lord rejoice.
Look to the Lord and his strength;
seek his face always.
Remember the wonders he has done,
his miracles, and the judgements he pronounced,
O descendants of Israel his servant,
O sons of Jacob, his chosen ones.
He is the Lord our God;
his judgements are in all the earth."

(1 Chronicles 16:8-14) [Italics mine]

Perhaps God is waiting for us to praise him like that, and to pray for revival in the knowledge of what it may mean in terms of judgement for believers and those who will come to faith, as well as for those who reject God's ways. As we pray in *faith* in this way, but always in *love*, with an eternal perspective (*hope*), that any means God chooses to use must be secondary if the end result is eternal life, then we shall be ready for the glorious but extremely difficult time ahead.

But how many will still want to pray for revival on those terms? Will we persevere through judgement to glory? Or will the beginnings of revival founder on the rock of our disillusionment, as we see the way God has to work in the West and Western Church? Are we those who are full of false optimism, or do we recognise that the West has already fallen prey to a major deceit: the darkness of an age old "New Age"? Conceived in the East, but birthed in the West, it will eventually spread throughout the world. We are all in danger.

CHAPTER TWO

New Age Deceit

I had what many today would describe as a "New Age" experience, long before the term was popularised. Many years ago when I was a student in London, a number of us would go for a jog in the evening round the "Inner Circle" of Regent's Park. On one occasion, I paused on the bridge overlooking the lake as the others went back to college. It was a warm evening, permeated with that special scent of flowers, foliage and grass after a light shower of rain. The moon was reflected in the water. The sound of traffic, not so heavy in those days, was muffled, a faint roar in the distance.

Suddenly it seemed as if everything in nature came alive in a fascinating way. The moon, stars, trees, flowers and water were vibrant, throbbing with mysterious power. It was as if they were calling out to me, and there was that within me which longed to respond. I felt that somehow I could merge with nature, we would be one, in some sort of mystical experience. Whether this happened in a moment, or longer, I do not remember. But then came the still small voice of the Holy Spirit, which I knew so well, warning me of danger. I drew back from the brink and the experience passed. It was only later that I analysed it as a temptation to become involved in pantheism – that god is everything and everything is god, and that the "god" in every human being can merge with god in nature, ultimately achieving a state of bliss. How different from an objective, transcendent yet personal God, over against man, yet who chooses to dwell within those who humble themselves. In pantheism there is no cross, no repentance; just self-fulfilment, conditional perhaps only on our right attitude to the environment, to nature. This is now a major feature of the New Age movement.

It is so easy for Christians, alert to the dangers of the occult, to appear negative about every aspect of new teaching. We need to reaffirm, loud and clear, that we are interested in conservation, ecology and have a positive attitude to our beautiful planet. I have so many memories of wholesome experiences of nature and anticipate many more to come. Beautiful views; glorious sunsets; the roar of waves dashing onto rocks on a Cornish beach; the fascination of the wilderness around the Dead Sea; the vastness of the Pacific Ocean; an active volcano seen from the air. The wind in my hair, the air like wine, the sheer sense of freedom, climbing the Lake District fells. The gratitude, spoken or silent, to the God who created it all in lavish abundance, for us to enjoy and use wisely. Instead, much has been spoilt, but that is not remedied by worship of the creature rather than the Creator. Many who become concerned about conservation are drawn almost unawares into a sense of reverence for nature which can so easily be exploited by those who overtly worship it.

So often this is linked with a revival of respect for cultures very different from our own. Christians would want to affirm this positive interest, without falling into the trap of moving from respect to acceptance, leading to affirmation of the *religion* which may be interwoven with that culture. Are Christians discerning enough to avoid this pitfall, and courageous enough to risk even being blamed as racist – when nothing is further from our hearts – as we seek to respect different peoples, show interest in their traditions, but avoid compromise over religion?

World Magazine, with its excellent articles on conservation issues, recently included a major supplement on the Coburg Peninsula and Seven Spirit Bay, an Aboriginal homeland in Australia's Northern Territory. An advert for holiday-makers typifies the way in which many conservationists and those making money from tourism connected with conservation projects, are learning to use the subtle, semi-religious language of the New Age. In the legends of Aborigines, the Coburg Peninsula is where the Mother of the Earth first stepped on Australia back in the Dreamtime, and began her long journeys, singing the land to life. There is no more sacred place. The advertisement informs us in pictures and words, that lightning awakens the earth, and the drama of the cycle of seven seasons at Seven Spirit Bay begins again. After lightning, ''Thundering empowers the Earth. Rainmaking feeds the Earth. Greening is the celebration of the Earth. Windstorming enlivens the Earth. Fire-raging purifies the Earth. Cloudless Blue is the waiting of the Earth . . . You'll come to know about the seven seasons in the Aboriginal calendar . . . You'll live through a series of wonderful natural adventures and cultural encounters. And you will experience the great indefinable feeling that we call 'power of place' . . . Where nature and human nature are reconciled

. . . Coburg Peninsula is among the most beautiful dry tropical coastal wilderness areas on Earth. Even to meet nothing here is a rich experience for that 'nothing' is a great silence coloured with deep intensity . . . it is the presence of the spirit of this land. To imagine that there are meanings and personality in the wilderness is the ancient nature of the 'Dreaming', the spiritual heritage of Australia's aboriginal people. Whether the dreaming is done by the land or person is inconsequential, as essentially the two become inseparable. Wild places, where they survive, communicate silently with our inner senses, creating strong feelings and evoking impressions of power and depth beyond ordinary logic. The experience of wilderness is always highly individualised and deeply personal, it emanates from a subjective and vibrant relationship that is edifying and inspiring. This is the power of place, and power of place is what you will experience at Seven Spirit Bay.''

A New Age view of history

This is seductive language, appealing to the mystical side of our nature. The New Ager would see man as evolving spiritually as well as in other ways, and yet claim there is a naturally supernatural cycle about the whole process. So, man is a religious animal and, they claim, the "natural" religion for man is a mixture of pantheism (in its crude form, worship of many gods, but in its deeper sense, the worship of god as all and all as god) and animism (the worship of nature spirits). These religions achieved more highly developed forms in the East, in Hinduism, Buddhism, etc. But as mankind was developing in other ways, settling in cities, fortifying

26

them, conquering others, so kingdoms and empires were formed (almost always male-dominated and defended or enlarged by men through war). At the same time the first great monotheistic religion developed – Judaism, with its view of the great (male) King and only God. Then, arising from it, but spurned by it, Christianity emerged, to dominate the world for 2000 years, only to be rejected, in the Middle East particularly, by Islam. Wars were increasingly caused by strife between or even within Christianity and Islam. Later came the great explosion of cultural development in the Renaissance, in the arts and science. Discoveries in the latter led us through the Industrial Revolution to the Technological Revolution with two world wars in between. In the Cold War following, there was stalemate. With all our brilliance, we had succeeded in developing nuclear weapons and so kept each other at bay – but at great cost, in more ways than one. Yet despite many positive scientific discoveries, man with all his knowledge and development in other ways was unable to solve basic problems like world poverty. The final straw was when it was discovered and generally acknowledged in the late 1980s, that through many of our own scientific achievements we were actually destroying our own planet, not just by wars and the ugly blots on the landscape of dirty cities and their waste, but through global warming caused by our own actions.

Now according to the New Agers, we are moving out of the astrological Age of Pisces, the Christian era, into the Age of Aquarius. It will not be an easy path, but the goals of this Age are peace, unity and harmony with nature. There should not be so much an overturning of all that has gone before, but harmonisation of all that is good in science, culture and religion. We need in scientific enquiry to concentrate on saving the planet and feeding mankind. We need, say the New Agers, to affirm the best in every culture and religion, leaving aside that which divides, and has even caused war, and looking for that which unites. We need to move away from strife-ridden male domination and rediscover the feminine principle prevalent so often in primitive religion. The secret of it all is to recognise the powers for good within ourselves, in fact, the power of god. As we do that we shall discover that all the time we are really at one with the same god in nature, as in the belief of the ancient "natural" religions of man. But with the benefit of later insights, according to New Age teaching, we now know that the god we discover is really the Christ-spirit, which has been manifested under different names – Jesus, Buddha, etc. – but who will be revealed to us in an Ultimate Manifestation by Spiritual Masters (akin to elevated spirit guides). There will be world government with due recognition of national and cultural distinctiveness. Because there are many difficulties in the way, gradual evolution of our thinking is no longer sufficient. We need a "quantum leap" of consciousness on the part of mankind. This will be achieved as more and more people tune into the mystical forces of the universe, through meditation and other means. At last we shall be in harmony with one another, with nature and with God – for all is god and god is all, and the supreme manifestation of god will enlighten us all.

How different from a Christian view of history, culture, God and man. It is also important to realise that not all New Agers have this overview – it is not a

28

homogeneous humanly organised movement. There are now recognised New Age authors, New Age experts in all kinds of fields including politics, different branches of science, religion, the arts. There is a directory of New Age organisations and a deliberate attempt at "networking" – working in a loose-knit association with the same general purpose in view. But a typical man-in-the-street New Ager may have little idea or even desire for world government, and know nothing about spiritual masters, but may be deeply into yoga, transcendental meditation, and possibly an unconscious pantheism in his involvement in an ecology movement. Another might attend church regularly, take part in an interfaith celebration of creation at his cathedral and applaud the Pope praying for peace with people of all faiths at Assisi, where St Francis taught us how to commune with nature. Yet another might live for a while in the New Age Findhorn community in Scotland, be overtly into occult practices and consciously equate the god within the devil, whom he regards as falsely maligned as evil.

The threat of the New Age

The New Age movement is like nothing we have ever seen before in history, in terms of the breadth of its appeal, its rapid spread throughout the world in little more than a decade, and the measure of its success in already transforming the consciousness of millions of people. I believe it to be the main force opposing true Christianity and a far greater threat in terms of its appeal to the soul of man than a religion like Islam. We shall find the task of evangelism increasingly difficult where men and women have been influenced by the New Age, but even more dangerous is the way it is infiltrating and so undermining Christianity. Christians with liberal views will be the first to fall prey, but those with traditional views and those who are renewed are in danger too.

Other Christian writers have analysed in depth the different strands woven into the New Age, from spiritualism to Eastern religions. They have shown the vulnerability particularly of the West, which opened its doors in the sixties to drugs, "flower power" and all things occult. But New Age teaching is much more "respectable" and it is important to understand that it seems to be permeating so many aspects of Western life.

Alternative medicine

Medicine is one of these areas, and no less a person than Prince Charles himself has given respectability to alternative medicine. Whereas many aspects of this may well be wholesome, the discerning Christian will recognise those therapies which have occult characteristics, and which are causing thousands to be vulnerable to New Age philosophies. Prince Charles's speech delivered to the British Medical Association on 14th December 1982 can be seen today as the turning point for what is now promoted and marketed as alternative medicine. He criticised the BMA for encouraging the estrangement of science from nature and harming patients by viewing the body as a mere machine. There is so much in the speech that many Christians would applaud, until the Prince went on to commend Paracelsus, the sixteenth-century German physician who believed in an occult cosmic unity. "Through the centuries," said the Prince, "healing has been practised by faith healers who are guided by traditional wisdom that sees illness as a disorder of the whole person, involving not only the patient's body, but his mind, his self-image, his dependence on the physical and social environment, as well as his relation to the cosmos." The following year the Prince shared a platform at the Bristol Cancer Help Centre with Dr Alec Forbes, director of the Centre. My information on this comes from John Dale's book *The Prince and the Paranormal* (published by W.H. Allen & Co. of Star). Dr Forbes is a Fellow of the Royal College of Physicians (London) and Doctor of Medicine (Oxon.). However, John Dale maintains "a number of doctors . . . despite Forbes's undoubted skills . . . held that in some respects he was a crank." But he found unexpected support from Prince Charles, who accepted the invitation to attend the opening ceremony of the Centre and in his speech spoke approvingly of some of Forbes's methods. "It may be described as psychotherapy, or religion, or the power of prayer, or whatever – but it represents that invisible aspect of the universe which, although unprovable in terms of orthodox science, as man has devised it, nevertheless cries out for us to keep our minds as open as possible and not to dismiss it as mere hocus-pocus." Much good work is done at the Centre, mainly using orthodox methods. But the brochure for the Centre states that "healing by touch, sometimes called spiritual healing, is available". Many Christians, although they may believe in prayer for healing in the name of Jesus, will be disturbed to learn that, according to John Dale, Forbes's beliefs include spiritualism, astrology and reincarnation. He has written in his book *Try Being Healthy* (Langdon Books) of psychic surgery and radionics (use of a pendulum for diagnosis over, e.g., a sample of hair of a patient), to name just some of a number of occult techniques which he describes with approval, although they are not overtly practised at the Bristol Centre. Prince Charles must have been aware of this, but perhaps unaware at the time of damage to his future role as Defender of the (Christian) faith.

Western man is so obsessed with pursuit of health and healthy living that he is vulnerable to any method, however bizarre, which appears to achieve the desired result. Scientifically controlled experiments often show that the results are favourable but are unable to determine why the method works. In Britain we can in some instances have alternative medicine on the National Health. A senior nurse told me she had left a well-known London Teaching Hospital because she had been ostracised for opposing Buddhist techniques taught to expectant mothers to help in childbirth, whereas there was opposition to orthodox Christian prayer for healing. In private practice, seemingly inexplicable, strange treatments are advertised openly and practised by "professionals". Many therapies concentrate the mind on the hidden power within – and so New Age philosophy takes root.

Techniques of meditation

It is not just those suffering from ill-health who are vulnerable. Men and women, recognising that materialism does not satisfy, are turning for fulfilment to methods of meditation which claim to raise our level of consciousness and lead to a release of our supposed inherent divine powers. First popularised by the Beatles, techniques like Transcendental Meditation have spread like wildfire. Many go to the East in search of religious experience. In 1989 *fifteen million* people descended on Allahabad in India for a special festival, to learn from the samnyasins or holy men. They teach yoga and other spiritual practices to attain liberation. One samnyasin is quoted in the *World Magazine* article "Seekers of Emptiness" by Tim Malyon (November 1989): "We have only one question . . . What is I? . . . the answer . . . He is everyone, he is everywhere, one in the universe, one in existence . . . He is you, You-in-You, U-nion. That is he. Sometimes we hold our body in one position, sitting with that thought. Then we do practice, following the breathing, deeper and deeper. Then everything stops – that is realisation. Everything comes to a point . . . you are thoughtless, if there is no question in the body any more, then there is no breathing – nothing."

Tim Malyon goes on to say, "Both Hindu and Buddhist renouncers search for release from the eternal road of life, death and rebirth. . . . The samnyasins' methods are many and varied: bodily subjugation, breathing and body yoga, meditation and visualization, intellectual and emotional insight, and *bhakti*, ecstatic devotion to and immersion in such godheads as Lord Shiva. These naked or saffron-robed practitioners, painted and wild, may seem bizarre, even frightening to the outsider. But their methods, developed over centuries, are of increasing interest to the West.

"Consciousness-raising groups are spreading fast.

Psychotherapeutic experiences offering release from unconscious drives are no longer the resource of the so-called sick . . . Psychologists have been studying the experience of oneness . . . such experiences, once they occur, seem to be psychologically healthy, even foils against depression, leading to intense feelings of optimism and life affirmation.''

It is not just the Far East and the West which are vulnerable. I heard on the news programmes on 13th October 1989, just before the Iron Curtain was torn open, that the ''Psychotherapy Craze'' was even sweeping Russia. Germady Gerasimov, Soviet spokesman, was unable to explain it, but announced it had the blessing of the Minister of Health. Two Soviet ''healers'' in particular were featured, one who uses mystical hand movements, the other who is able to influence the health of those viewing him on television. Miracles take place. There are religious overtones to the craze, indicating that the deep mystical trend in Russian society was not killed off in 1917. What, I wonder, will fill the void now left after Communism?

In our own country, the Lancashire town of Skelmersdale was reported on the Channel 4 television programme *Not on a Sunday* as being the unlikely centre for about 350 people who have moved to the same area for the purpose of practising transcendental meditation. They are observing its effect not just on the individual, but society. There are T.M. centres in factories and businesses based on T.M. principles. Everyone on the programme appeared to exude a sense of well-being and happiness. Only the TV interviewer seemed to find it odd and rather amusing when suddenly, as a group of apparently normal people were sitting meditating, some of them "took off" and hopped over the cushioned floor, still in a sitting position, apparently in a state of ecstasy, in some altered state of consciousness. I would like to think that viewers found it either amusing or sad, but I suspect that years of watching New Age TV fiction may have blunted the common sense of many.

Infiltration of society

Even fashion has been influenced, according to Kate Saunders in a *Sunday Times* feature on 29th October 1989. I quote at length because the article shows great perception: "A New Age is dawning – the age, according to believers, in which the heartless materialists of the Eighties will be transformed into the caring global citizens of the Nineties. 'New Age' is the generic term for the explosion of interest in ecology and all things alternative – mystical religion, healing, mind-expanding psychobabble . . . Last year's smart woman . . . next year . . . will be a spiritual creature in a simple white robe, empathising over a pottery mug of herbal tea. Around her neck will hang a crystal, and not just for ornament. Crystals, it is claimed, can improve meditation, restore inner peace. . . . [The article features a large photograph of a family in 'New Age' clothes.] Basically the New Age person is into consciousness raising, caring and green politics. Hundreds of ideologies, from rebirthing therapy to the Tarot, come under the New Age umbrella. Really dedicated New Agers believe they are all plugged into the same source of spiritual power which will unite the whole world by 2000. Mikhail Gorbachev is a New Age hero because he is working to melt down the Iron Curtain and eliminate the bad *karma* between the superpowers. Prince Charles is our New Age royalty, chatting to plants and striking out against impersonal modernist architecture. The Bishop of Durham is a churchman for the New Age with his definition of God as 'the power behind things . . . who is constantly making for love, righteousness and peace'. Not that conventional Christianity has much of a place in the New Age. The doctrine that God is a separate force from mankind is definitely old hat. New Agers feel we are all potentially god-like.''

Perhaps the final confirmation that the ''New Age'' had arrived on the scene in the UK was when it was mentioned in the longest-running serial on radio, ''The Archers''! Linda Snell speculated in an episode in January 1990 that the New Age had probably originated in Ambridge! Advertisements, too, reflect interest in the New Age. Nissan Cars, who had used status symbol adverts in the 80s, began, according to a Channel 4 programme, to use research into our ''Zen spots'', with the aim of producing an advert which makes us relax and connect up to the environment. The idea is that the viewer will feel at one with the car, and the driver and car are depicted as at one with the world around us. Many management training courses also include New Age ideas and practices. The Trustees Savings Bank actively promoted the New Age in its youth magazine in the Spring of 1990, but apologised after massive Christian protest organised by my husband.

The New Age: an idea leading to a revolution

We have only had space for an overview of New Age thinking and the way it is infiltrating society the world over. I heard that one leading evangelical had dismissed it as a ''passing fad'', but I believe that to be a complete misunderstanding of the forces at work in the world today. An idea can lead to a revolution when the time is right. The entire consciousness of man is at present being revolutionised as old certainties are shattered. Despite the Chernobyl accident, politicians were still trying to reassure the cynical public that better designed nuclear power stations were safe – until research revealed in 1990 that, as everyone suspected, the higher incidence of leukaemia in children living near power stations is probably linked to their fathers' working there. That together with the Bhopal disaster of 1984, when 2000 people were killed by the escape of cyanide gas from a multi-national company factory, shattered man's confidence of being able to control his scientific inventions. The terrible famines in Ethiopia, together with the discovery of the greenhouse effect, given credence as a theory by Mrs Thatcher in a speech to the Royal Society in 1988, showed us that some of those inventions were leading to planet earth being out of control. Then political certainties vanished with the disintegration of the Communist bloc. Euphoria gave way to apprehension as new governments formed were in turn overthrown. Economic systems appear to be incapable of finding solutions to the problem of inflation. Despite the upsurge of nationalism, there is increasing awareness that we may not be able to survive as independent nation states. Scientists, environmentalists, economists, politicians, all appear to be recognising the need for worldwide co-operation. It will only take what Dr W. Broecker, a leading American climatologist, has called "unpleasant surprises in the greenhouse", e.g. even worse major hurricanes, droughts, floods, etc., worldwide, to force that co-operation upon us.

Everything which stands in the way of that co-operation will be increasingly vilified. Terrorism and aggressive nationalism are already condemned, although doubtless there will be further tragedies and wars caused by those who pursue their own ends. As a result the world will look for a key to transform the consciousness of mankind to bring about not only desire for, but actual unity, harmony and peace. The New Agers will say they have the key, and it carries the added bonus that the transformation can take place all the more rapidly as we unleash the amazing power of the god within, particularly when we learn to "network" with those of like mind all over the world and even with the earth itself.

Problems in the monotheistic religions

Another factor of far-reaching importance in the world today in bringing the New Age of age, is what has happened recently in the three major monotheistic religions. The extraordinary phenomenon of anti-semitism, manifested since the days of Queen Esther of Old Testament fame, is rearing its ugly head yet again. The unceasing unrest connected with the state of Israel, and brought to a head by the Palestinian "Intifada", inflames this ugly passion. The unwillingness of Israeli leaders to negotiate with the PLO appears to much of the rest of the world as meaningless intransigence, a threat to peace not only in the Middle East but worldwide. Jews, because they are "different", are again being treated as scapegoats in situations where other factors altogether are the cause of discontent. Although many Jews are agnostic, yet in the eyes of Gentiles they are inseparably linked with Judaism, and so it is their religion which, perhaps subconsciously, is blamed.

Islamic fundamentalism, leading during the regime of the Ayatollah Khomeini to seizure of American hostages, violence in the embassy in Britain, other terrorist activities, escalation of the war in Lebanon, death threats against Salman Rushdie, and fuelling the war mongering ambitions of President Saddam Hussein of Iraq, is a force in the world which is feared and hated by lovers of peace. It is very significant that the term "fundamentalist" is now used in a derogatory way, and fundamentalists of very different religions are regarded by others as tarred with the same brush.

In Christianity, we should not under-estimate the damage done by the downfall of some tele-evangelists. The United States took over the role of Britain as the base for world-wide missionary activity (a role rapidly passing to countries in the Far East). It is a country of extremes, where high rates of violence and drug-taking co-exist with a church attendance of nearly fifty per cent. Extremes within the Christian religion, too, range from outrageous liberalism in the episcopal church, to what some onlookers would regard as brash "born again" fundamentalism. Many millions take their religion in pre-packaged form via one or other of the numerous television channels. This can produce a low-cost, low-involvement Christianity, high on sentimentalism and sensationalism. There is little safeguard for the vulnerable and gullible. In a country where New Age philosophy is spreading like wildfire, what protection is there for those viewers whose idols have toppled from their pedestals? More conservative Christians will deplore the immorality of some tele-evangelists, their methods and their "prosperity gospel", and be deeply concerned lest their message, which did convey the Gospel, be rejected along with the fallen preachers.

I believe that not only is that bound to be the case with significant numbers of folk, leaving them with a void waiting to be filled, but it also adds fuel to the fire of deep-seated suspicion of "fundamentalists". All are branded together, and although a thoughtful Christian who has a firm belief in the Bible as the inspired Word of God might be miles apart from a hard-sell prosperity gospel preacher, and poles apart from an Islamic fundamentalist, yet in the eyes of increasing numbers the word spells trouble.

Interfaith influence

As a result of these disturbing events connected with the monotheistic religions, there is an increasing pressure not only to react against the "fundamentalism" within each of them, but to support religious leaders who were already exploring interfaith relationships.

Although I had known that for some time bodies like the World Council of Churches had been moving far beyond ecumenical discussions, into exploring "dialogue'' between the faiths, it came home to me when I had to lead a Women's World Day of Prayer service in 1981. The theme was ''The Earth is the Lord's'' and the service was prepared by Christian American Indian women. There was a dialogue in which the earth was personified and addressed as ''Mother'' and God was called ''Great Spirit''. I was sufficiently perturbed by that and other aspects to alter the service which I led. It is a short step from syncretistic language to interfaith events. 1993 has been declared a Year of Religious Understanding by four international interfaith organisations. 1993 is the centenary of the World Parliament of Religions which first met in Chicago, regarded as the start of the Interfaith Movement. We shall doubtless see a great increase this decade in interfaith activity, the basis tenet of which is that the same God is worshipped in all the great world religions. Once that is accepted, bearing in mind the pantheistic nature of religions such as Hinduism and Buddhism, there is an open door for infiltration of New Age (and age-old) beliefs into Christianity. The World Wide Fund for Nature, which quite naturally regards it as vital to seek the co-operation of all the great religions in its aim of conservation, has become an important vehicle for organising major interfaith events with an emphasis on our attitude to the earth. Some of these events have been alarming, not only with respect to the compromise of the Christian message, but in introducing worshippers to New Age views.

This is why I do not get too excited about statistics showing a turn of the tide in church attendance. An Interfaith, New Age mish-mash will be quite palatable to millions of people, apparently satisfying their religious yearnings. We shall examine later the dangers of the Interfaith movement in itself, but looking at it now as an aspect of the New Age movement, we need to assess the whole phenomenon from a Christian viewpoint.

A Christian view of the New Age

I find it fascinating that the first temptation ever to assail the mind of a human being, was to substitute in place of God's word the belief that secret knowledge was available, which would cause the eyes of the first man and woman to "be opened and ye shall be as gods, knowing good and evil" (Genesis 3:5, A.V. The Hebrew can have either a plural or a singular reference – "You will be like God" N.I.V.) The whole realm of the occult is of course concerned with the discovery, by using special techniques, of secret knowledge and powers, which can be manipulated for one's own end, and to wield influence (good or bad) over others. But New Age religious views are taking us back to the very essence of original sin.

There are many points of entry into the New Age movement (including alternative medicine, interfaith worship, some aspects of the conservation movement) and vast numbers of people will move through those doors. Some will enter just out of curiosity, or to experience something above and beyond the mundane. Others will be in serious pursuit of health, or world harmony or the salvation of planet earth. Yet others will be in search of occult powers. Most will recognise sooner or later man's inability to change his personal life or his world by normal human methods. At that point comes the temptation to "be as gods", using all kinds of techniques, from forkbending to witchcraft, to develop the necessary power.

I believe that the movement is apparently succeeding because, whatever human organisations might be involved, it is Satanically manipulated. It would have failed long ago if the various techniques did not work. But the inescapable fact is that so often they do. People *are* healed through occult therapies; relaxation and a sense of peace *can* be achieved through Transcendental Meditation; interfaith worship *does* lead to greater harmony; communing with nature *does* help in horticulture and agriculture. The pace of world events must seem to corroborate that we are at a turning point in history and gives credence to the Age of Aquarius teaching.

The conclusion which millions will draw is that we are god and that divine power, released through human beings or in nature, by whatever means, whether meeting to meditate at the intersection of ley lines or tapping into similar forces in the human body or mind, will solve all our problems. I believe that the power that men and women are tapping and unleashing, whether knowingly or not, is no god within but the power of Satan and his demons.

When we consider that there are already one billion Hindus and Buddhists in the world, and that millions more are influenced by them; that the USSR is now wide open to all kinds of philosophies; that there is a so-called post-Christian vacuum in the West and Westernised nations with millions already involved in aspects of the New Age, perhaps we begin to realise just what a serious situation has developed in the world. The whole scene of contemporary or "pop" music, which affects so many millions, has been deeply infiltrated by the New Age. For example, the annual Festival at Glastonbury, which attracts a quarter of a million people, is now virtually a breeding ground for New Age ideas.

Not only does this teaching go back to the original sin in Genesis, but I am convinced the New Age movement has all the hall-marks of the Rebellion which is described in the Bible as the characteristic of the Last Days before the Return of Christ — the Rebellion against the God revealed in the Bible through Jesus Christ alone, the God who is transcendent yet immanent, who is totally Other yet who will, by the Holy Spirit, make human beings his temple. He is holy, we are sinful and "without the shedding of blood there is no forgiveness" (Hebrews 9:22). The requirements of justice and love are met in the Cross of Christ, so that where there is repentance "whoever believes in him shall not perish but have eternal life" (John 3:16).

What could be less popular in the West today than the concepts of holiness, sin, repentance, substitutionary atonement (Jesus having borne God's wrath for our sin), commitment to God, belief in his Son as the *only* way of salvation, and judgement for those who do not repent?

Once it is recognised that the very essence of the New Age movement is rebellion against the true God, and consequent unleashing of Satanic power, then verses from 2 Thessalonians 2:1–12 have amazing relevance: "Concerning the coming of our Lord Jesus Christ and our being gathered to him . . . Don't let anyone deceive you in any way, for that day will not come until the rebellion occurs and the man of lawlessness is revealed, the man doomed to destruction. . . . And then the lawless one will be revealed, whom the Lord Jesus will overthrow with the breath of his mouth and destroy by the splendour of his coming. The coming of the lawless one will be in accordance with the work of Satan displayed in all kinds of counterfeit miracles, signs and wonders, and in every sort of evil that deceives those who are perishing. They perish because they refused to love the truth and so be saved. For this reason God sends them a powerful delusion so that they will believe the lie, and so that all will be condemned who have not believed the truth but have delighted in wickedness.''

''The lie'', I believe, is the original lie of the Tempter in the book of Genesis. The man of lawlessness can, as often in prophecy, have more than one fulfilment – interim and ultimate. As St John puts it in 1 John 4:3, ''Every spirit that does not acknowledge Jesus is not from God. This is the spirit of the Antichrist, which you have heard is coming and even now is already in the world.''

So it would appear that everyone who believes in the god within is manifesting the spirit of antichrist, but there will be an ultimate manifestation – Satan incarnate. The inner circle of New Agers of course refer to this as the Christ spirit. They believe Buddha, Jesus and other spiritual leaders revealed this spirit, the god within, in a purer way than most people. But the ultimate manifestation, they say, is soon be be revealed in one being. They call him Christ (and they do not mean Jesus). Christians should call him Antichrist.

Christianity faces its greatest challenge ever as the battle lines are drawn. Jesus has already won the victory but the task of the Church is to apply that victory in the world today, not just in defence of the faith, but in pushing back the powers of darkness. Anyone who sits loose to the Word of God will not be able to counteract the terrible deceit of these days. But what of evangelicals who profess to believe in the divine inspiration of the Bible? How ready are we to face the challenge of the New Age?

CHAPTER THREE

Evangelical Compromise

It is becoming commonplace to read in Christian newspapers and magazines statements such as: "Evangelical bishop invites the Bishop of Durham to lead his diocesan clergy conference"; "Four out of seven members of the commission responsible for liberal report on homosexuality are evangelicals"; and "Leading evangelical theologian offers cautious welcome to interfaith worship."

As evangelicals form an increasingly large grouping within the Church of England, and Anglican evangelicals are influential in wider evangelical circles, whatever happens within their ranks is bound to be of lasting significance to evangelicalism as a whole as well as to the Church of England. Probably the majority of evangelical scholars and theologians in England come from within the ranks of the Anglican church, many of them products of several thriving evangelical Anglican theological colleges. Sadly, in my view, increasing numbers of Anglican evangelicals are in grave danger of compromise, and to some extent are unaware of the enormous pressures leading to that compromise.

Fundamentalist evangelicals

I would distinguish three main strands within evangelicalism, although of course there is overlap

47

between each. One grouping, which would scarcely figure at all amongst Anglicans, would be the simplistic fundamentalists. Hopefully, there are no longer any ''flat earthers'', but there are many who believe in the inerrancy of Scripture in a completely literal way. To them, the seven days of creation *have* to be seven literal days. If there are two similar stories in the gospels about blind men being healed, one referring to two men and the other to one, the simplistic fundamentalist would maintain we are dealing with two different incidents. (Other evangelicals would see them as two accounts of the same incident, accurate from the point of view of the memory of the two eye witnesses. If eye witnesses vary slightly, for that to be recorded is more realistic than for the Holy Spirit to smooth over all the differences.) Such simplistic faith should never be despised. There are those to whom God has given an unquestioning faith which others should not attempt to undermine. However, this type of evangelicalism was, surprisingly, predominant in Christian Union circles in universities in the 1950s. The unfortunate consequence was that some Christians reacted against it and went to other extremes. Two well-known liberals, the Archbishop of York and the Bishop of Durham, were adversely affected by this rather anti-intellectual fundamentalism, and tend to regard most evangelicals as holding this position.

Conservative evangelicals

The second and by far the largest grouping would be the conservative evangelicals. An editorial in the *Church of England Newspaper* several years ago expressed something of this view: "What are we to make of the inerrancy debate about the Bible? . . . Do we believe that the Bible is infallible or not? Most certainly! It will never lead any of us astray; its message consistently and 'unerringly' leads us to Christ, God's final revelation to the world . . . it provides the only reliable standard for belief and practice . . . . When questions about Inerrancy are asked, however, further questions need to be put. Are we speaking of historical, scientific, mathematical or journalistic standards of inerrancy? . . . (e.g.) with the history of the Bible. Are we looking for an exact blow-by-blow chronology of events? No. 'True historical genius', writes Sir William Ramsay, 'lies in selecting the great crises, the great agents and the great movements. . . . The historian may dismiss years with a word, and devote considerable space to a single incident.' Thus the Bible will disappoint those who are hoping for a chronological record of all the Pharaohs of Egypt, because this is highly selective, *interpreted* history. But it is certainly not erroneous. It's the same with that much disputed battleground – Genesis. Could this ever have been a journalistic account? Or a 'scientific' account? Certainly not. Here is a magnificent, timeless, religious explanation of our beginnings. It . . . does not conflict with the findings of science – as R.J. Berry, Professor of Genetics in London University, helpfully pointed out."

Liberal evangelicals

The third grouping is liberal evangelicalism. They vary in their views but by and large would seek to be definite in preaching the Gospel, but are very vague when it comes to a view of Scripture, finding embarrassment with large sections of it. I believe they are pulling the rug out from beneath both evangelicalism and evangelism, and are closer to true liberals in their thinking.

It is important to stress that there are conservative evangelicals like myself who have arrived at this position after thinking through and sometimes agonising over many complex issues. Yet I had suspected for some time that liberal churchmen regarded themselves as having a monopoly on the ability to think deeply about theological issues, to question and to doubt. Not only that, but they were beginning to raise doubt to the level of a virtue, whereas certainty about any aspect of truth was being written off as unthinking fundamentalism.

This was confirmed when I read the Bishop of Oxford's review of David Hare's play about the Church of England, *Racing Demon*, launched at the National Theatre in February 1990. I later went to see the play. It is brilliant, witty, at times perceptive, at times somewhat inaccurate in capturing the inner workings of the Church of England. The most unlikely part of the plot is when an evangelical curate (who is caricatured as going over the top) is aided and abetted by a bishop in an attempt to get rid of a totally ineffectual liberal clergyman. (In real life it would be far more likely to be the other way round!) The curate longs for people to be converted, believes in an intervening God who can cure people even of AIDS, and wants a full church. Richard Harries, the Bishop of Oxford, comments: ''In contrast to all this, there is just the suggestion of the possibility of a true God . . . Lionel (the liberal clergyman), for all his hesitancy and diffidence, is also struggling to explore and convey the divine mystery. On aesthetic, moral and theological grounds, his plea is for a proper, reverent reticence in our dealings with the divine.'' Not only had the bishop totally failed to notice that the depiction of the evangelical was a caricature, but he appeared to regard as laudable the liberal clergyman's disastrously inept efforts in e.g. pastoral care. Somehow, I cannot imagine Jesus applauding a clergyman for being diffident in even suggesting the possibility of a God!

I used to wonder why it was that liberal bishops did not seem interested in analysing why growing, thriving churches, which are nearly always evangelical (and often charismatic), are so healthy. Now I realise that they are unimpressed by ''success'', even true success measured in terms of spiritual reality. ''Exploration'' replaces evangelism, doubt and failure are highly regarded, and mistakenly identified as at the heart of Christianity (in contrast to the true heart, which is the victory of the Resurrection over the apparent defeat of the Cross).

Unfortunately, in reaction to this liberal exaltation of doubt, there are those evangelicals who go to the other extreme in regarding all doubt as sin. I think we do evangelicalism a disservice by such attitudes. We need to be more honest about our questioning, our doubting, our agonising, and show that we are able to think issues through on a deep level – in some cases coming through to deeper convictions; in some, living with unanswered questions.

An analysis of doubt

From my own experience, I have noticed three types of questioning over theological issues. I would identify the first as the *necessary* stage of doubt. This is almost inevitable for someone like myself who became a Christian as a young child. There is bound to come a time when one is more able to think issues through, and it is important to allow this to go deep, to ensure there is nothing second-hand about one's faith. For me, this stage took nearly ten years from when I was twenty-four. I was a member of a small clergy wives' group, one of whom had a Ph.D. in theology (Oxon). There was a psychiatrist, an R.E. teacher, and a social worker amongst others. They included an atheist, an agnostic, two liberals and two evangelicals. Our evenings were not "knit and natter" sessions, but in-depth discussions. At one point we studied Tillich. The "Ground of our Being" concept of God appealed to the mystical side of my nature. It was not long before I was doubting even the existence of God. I vividly remember tossing and turning at night, believing only that if there is a God, he is ultimate truth, and the most important thing in my life was to rediscover, if possible, that truth. I gradually came to a much deeper faith about all the major truths of Christianity. There was still uncertainty about some aspects of liberal theology and the Bible. The end of that necessary period of doubt came when one day I switched on the radio to hear a friend speak on the Christmas story. He had been one of my husband's theological lecturers, and had been an evangelical. I was distressed to hear him devote nearly an hour of peak listening time to "destroying" the Christmas narratives, rather than presenting the vital truths to his audience. What a missed opportunity! I recognised the snare of the pseudo-science of what used to be called "higher criticism", which actually requires as much "faith" as the evangelical view of divine inspiration; is based on prejudices such as unwillingness to accept that God would intervene in miracles, or reveal the future in prophecy; and creates confusion among Christians and non-Christians alike. Another example of necessary doubt would be when faced with an issue which has not previously been considered, such as what is God's attitude towards people of other faiths. It may be a long time before someone reaches an understanding of biblical truth about this.

The second type of doubt I would describe as *harmful*. Doubt can be a temptation which, if entertained, becomes the sin of unbelief. It falls into that category when God has spoken and we are unwilling to accept, or he shows us the necessity of trusting him through uncertainty over a particular issue, but we insist on entertaining the doubts to satisfy intellectual pride or to impress others.

I have hinted at the third type of doubt or questioning, when I referred to trusting God through uncertainty. This is a *deliberate* choice to leave a question mark over certain aspects of Christianity, which we cannot fully explain, but to maintain an attitude of basic trust. Many deep theological truths are to be found not in the resolution of all problems and questions, but in seeing God through them. Belief in God as Creator would be an example of that. One could believe firmly in the basic truth but it would be presumptuous to think we could ever answer all the questions about the details of the creative process. Other truths are perceived only when one is prepared to hold two complete opposites in tension – the Son of God as divine and human, the unity of the Trinity, election and predestination, righteousness in Christ and human failings, the love and wrath of God. Such an approach requires humility of the intellect rather than the arrogance of needing to win every argument.

The divine inspiration and human authorship of the Bible

My attitude to the Bible, which I believe to be a valid form of conservative evangelicalism, would be to hold in tension its divine inspiration and human authorship. Its sixty-six books were written by forty authors using three languages over 1600 years. None of the original manuscripts is available, although the 13,000 manuscripts we have, which show amazingly little variation between them, make it by far the best attested compilation of documents of its age in the world. Considering for the moment the human side of its origins, the unity of its message (the story of salvation) is quite extraordinary. It is simple, yet profound, and can be meaningful to the intellectual or the simple-minded. (Incidentally, the fact that the views of some liberal theologians are comprehensible *only* to the philosophically minded is, in my opinion, a mark of the spiritual poverty of those views, as that would never be the case with divine truth.) Although every jot and tittle are important, yet God, in his omniscience, knew that the Bible would be translated into numerous different languages, with all the nuances of interpretation which that makes possible, and that the original manuscripts would be lost. (Yet we know from comparing Dead Sea Scrolls with out later manuscripts, how painstaking the copying of scriptures was, and how before the Dead Sea Scrolls every scribe would have regarded it as of vital importance to be accurate. We know, too, that we can compare translations and gain a richness of understanding.)

I believe passionately that God to be known knew he had to make himself known – revelation was vital not only to counter the multiplicity of human opinions, but to enable the transcendent, almighty God to be known at all by mere mortals. Whereas God may be known in a general way through revelation in creation, he chose to make himself known in salvation through the person of his Son, so that the believer might have an eternal relationship with him. But how was this salvation story to be known? God knew (to put it simply) that writing was to be developed by, and in its turn would contribute to the development of, the earliest civilisations known to man. The earliest ''city-dwelling'' society was established in southern Mesopotamia 5000 years ago, where the oldest written inscription on clay tablets in the world (dated 3200 BC) has been found. In view of the vital significance of writing to man, God saw to it that there was eventually a complete written account of the way he intervened in history to make possible the salvation of man who was estranged from him through sin. Ultimate truths are expressed in the Bible in legal writing, history, poetry, prophecy, letters, theological treatise and apocalyptic literature. The whole is well and truly earthed in history, much of which had been corroborated archaeologically, and none of which has been disproved. I have just read recently that the latest excavations in Jericho have led to a re-dating of some ruins consistent with the biblical fall of Jericho. Future discoveries will no doubt throw light on other events. There will always be some unsolved questions. The thinking evangelical will hold to a firm belief in the power of divine inspiration working in and through the humanity of the biblical authors. The Holy Spirit did not correct the poor grammar of some authors such as Mark, or modify eyewitness accounts to make them tally exactly, which would be artificial, nor change the authors' view of the earth as flat with heaven above and hell below, but rather revealed absolute truth triumphing in and through human weakness. Whilst not finding it possible or even necessary to resolve every aspect, I would want to say loud and clear that the Bible is the word of God, and reveals ultimate truth. We can come to know that truth through encounter with Jesus, based on God's word in the Bible. We *can* be certain and proclaim that certainty.

Hermeneutics

A new factor on the Anglican evangelical scene in the last decade has been the emphasis on the so-called "science" of hermeneutics, to do with biblical interpretation. Basically, it assists the reader in arriving at the true meaning expressed in the words of the Bible. Textual, linguistic, cultural and historical studies aid in this process. All of this is important in helping with exegesis, which is the explanation of the biblical passage. Hermeneutics can play a vital role, but it is increasingly being used as an *excuse* by some evangelicals to explain away portions of the Bible. So in the debate over homosexuality, the true conservative evangelical would claim that the Bible clearly rules out homosexual practice. True liberals would ask us to pay far more attention to the plight of the homosexual than the teaching of the Bible. But because of the enormous pressure on Anglicans to be accepted as intellectually respectable, to keep in with the liberals and to be seen to err on the side of human sympathy rather than dogmatism, some evangelicals, including some who have been known as "conservatives", use hermeneutics to explain away the passages about homosexuality, as being relevant only to the situation of the writer's day. So, because it is known that all forms of debauchery and perversion were practised within the homosexual scene in the Roman Empire, the teaching on the subject in Romans chapter 1 would be regarded as condemning such excesses, rather than homosexual practice as such. Well-attested arguments against this interpretation are dismissed. This is the kind of reasoning which led to the extraordinary phenomenon of well-known evangelicals, in the majority on the Anglican Osborne Commission on homosexuality, producing a liberal report, leaked in early 1990. The report tends towards a lenient view of "faithful" practising homosexuals, recommends consideration of the "blessing" of their relationship, and moves towards a positive affirmation of practising homosexual clergy.

Hermeneutics, although valid in itself, is therefore increasingly used as perhaps a subconscious excuse for some evangelicals to move rapidly down the slippery slope of liberal theology. It is not in their hearts to dismiss Scripture, but slowly but surely more and more of its teaching is explained away. Although we read in 1 Corinthians 1 that the wisdom of scholars and philosophers is regarded as foolish, for "the foolishness of God is wiser than man's wisdom" (v. 25), we find that in place of proper humility towards divine revelation through the Bible there is pride in human intellectual processes. Reason or the dictates of human emotion are effectively regarded as more important than revelation, as evangelicals give in to the enormous pressures on them.

The necessity to uphold revelation

The battle for the minds of evangelicals is on. I am certainly no advocate of a mindless approach, but I do believe that we continually need to "be transformed by the renewing of [the] mind" (Romans 12:2). Satan is ruthless. He knows that if Christians concede ground over Scripture, they will in the end worship a god of their imagination rather than the God of revelation. They become wide open to all kinds of deceit.

This is the crossroads. We shall only be able to walk straight ahead along the narrow road with the word of God as "a lamp to [our] feet and a light for [our] path" (Psalm 119:105). If we compromise over revelation we shall be tempted to the left or right along the broad road, and discover many fellow travellers with whom there is a lot in common. These are nominal Christians, even church leaders who have never had a personal relationship with the living Christ. But because of the herd instinct and the desire for inclusiveness, it could seem natural to go along with them, not in order to point them back to the narrow road, but to keep them happy. There are people of other faiths, New Agers and a great multitude, all travelling along, unprepared for the way of the Cross.

In Action for Biblical Witness to Our Nation (ABWON), the organisation of which Tony and I are founders and co-directors, we are only too aware of the powerful onslaught on the mind to deviate from the way of revelation. Many who oppose Tony's stand in the General Synod of the Church of England, to uphold biblical theology and morality, tend to assume that he is an "unthinking fundamentalist". They know nothing of his continual agonising over issues. They are unaware of the intense pressure to conform, the deliberate attempts by the liberal establishment to woo him over, and when that failed, to discredit him; or of hurtful lack of support or even opposition from some fellow evangelicals, who seem blind to the issues at stake. There is the constant cry that we do not need prophetic pronouncements, but rather compassionate action. This leads us to continual self-examination, for if we are unloving then we deny the Gospel. If Tony says that homosexual practice, or other forms of immorality, are wrong, if he calls for the discipline of bishops who deny the fundamentals of the faith, if he proclaims that worship of Jesus is the only way to God and that people of other faiths need the Gospel, of course he *appears* unloving. It would be far easier to compromise. We are not homophobics, and the drip . . . drip of gay propaganda can get through, as it has to so many. Men like the Bishop of Durham and others have very pleasant personalities, and it can seem unkind to oppose their views. As for interfaith matters, it is a terrible prospect to think of millions without God and without hope in the world, unless they embrace the Gospel. It would be so much easier to concede first one aspect of biblical truth and then another, which is what so many have done, largely as a result of confusing human sympathy with divine love. What does it profit a Christian leader if he gains everyone's approval, but loses many souls? Which then is true love?

Time and time again we turn for strength to words such as those of Psalm 138:2. It reads, "You have exalted above all things your name and your word". I believe these words to be very significant. The name of God, the character and nature of God, God himself, is supreme over all, but the only way for human beings to know that, is through his word. God has spoken. We are foolish to ignore him. Without that revelation, it is your word against mine . . . and his . . . and hers. We sink in a morass of human opinion like the foolish man who built his house on the sand, compared with the wise man who built his house on the rock. He is the one "who comes to me and hears my words and puts them into practice", says the Lord in Luke 6:47.

God's word has never presented man with a soft option, yet many Anglican evangelicals would prefer that it did. The plea that it is all a matter of interpretation can so often be an excuse, for most of Scripture is plain in its meaning for all who have ears to hear, especially when it comes to central matters of doctrine and ethics. Before we look in more detail at areas of evangelical compromise, it is important to affirm those thousands of evangelicals within the Church of England and in other branches of the Church who are fervent in their adherence to Scripture, in their preaching of the Gospel, and in their support of those who take a stand over important issues.

The necessity to speak out against compromise

With the wholehearted support and prayer of our local
church and thousands of Christians, including many
who would not call themselves evangelicals, in and
beyond the UK, we have taken a stand in ABWON
over three main issues – doctrinal confusion, moral
confusion and interfaith compromise. But the support
from leading Anglican evangelicals, with one or two
notable exceptions, has been muted. We can therefore
illustrate from our own experience that there is serious
compromise within evangelicalism. The greatest clarity
from and unity amongst Anglican evangelicals was over
the controversy in 1984 and after about doctrinal issues.
They were absolutely clear on the bodily resurrection of
Christ (although unfortunately some liberal evangelicals were hazy about the virgin birth, because they felt
intellectually uncomfortable over the birth narratives in
two of the gospels). Many clergy wrote articles
defending these truths, scholars wrote books. But when
it came to any *action* being taken, the story was different.
It was thought to be not quite the done thing to oppose
the enthronement of a bishop, however heretical, and
rather extreme to persist until the doctrinal issues were
brought before the Church of England General Synod.
However, the evangelicals in Synod were pleased with
the end result in 1986 when the houses of clergy and
laity reaffirmed traditional beliefs by a large majority!
They congratulated Tony, David Holloway and others
for a successful outcome, even though they had not
given much support beforehand.

There remained the continuing mockery of not only
the Bishop of Durham (who at least has the honesty to

be completely open about his views) but other bishops too, remaining in office in which they are meant to uphold traditional belief and banish error, yet denying aspects of the creed. So when the Synod had a second chance to reaffirm the creeds in 1990 (which they did) Tony proposed an amendment ''that only those who uphold this traditional belief, including the virginal conception and bodily resurrection of Christ, should be eligible for or remain in episcopal or any other teaching office in the church''. After all, the vote to uphold the creeds would otherwise have no cutting edge. This amendment was overwhelmingly defeated, including by very many evangelicals. Yet Jesus and St Paul not only proclaimed the truth but spoke out in the strongest possible terms against those who confused or denied aspects of it, recommending discipline of such people. But because of a host of reasons – human sympathy, unwillingness to be unpopular, even to lose prospects of promotion, and not wishing to seem extreme, evangelicals by their voting compromised the scriptural teaching on discipline. Even worse, as a result of sympathy for the liberal bishops, they have been unloving to thousands of Christians and unbelievers who will remain confused. We have evangelical bishops, but it appears they prefer to act in ''collegiality'' as a house of bishops rather than take a stand. Occasionally one or two speak out, or reaffirm biblical truth in diocesan magazines, but hardly ever push publicly for anything to be *done*. Some have assured Tony they are working for the truth ''behind the scenes''. This may well be true – but where are the results? St Paul had to resist pressure publicly from St Peter at one point to compromise the Gospel. The gentle Barnabas was nearly led astray, but praise God that Paul stuck to his convictions and the Gospel of grace was preserved for posterity (Galatians 2:11-21).

A modern-day example of a courageous stand by an evangelical was seen in the (largely liberal) Episcopal Church of the United States. We witnessed the unseemly spectacle of Bishop Spong of Newark openly ordaining a practising homosexual priest, then having to climb down when the man turned out to be flagrant in advocating promiscuity. But an evangelical bishop (Terence Kelshaw) did have the courage publicly to denounce Bishop Spong's original action. The result was that the Presiding Bishop (Bishop Browning) issued an unprecedented statement: ''We decry the action by the Bishop of Newark . . . what is at stake is the discipline of the church . . . when persons move beyond the broad parameters of our common life . . . the seeds of anarchy are sown.'' In this case, a courageous stand of evangelical bishop against liberal bishop produced consequences of great benefit to the Church.

Yet in England, and I suspect elsewhere, there is a blockage in a large section of the evangelical world about the necessity not only to speak out for the truth, *but to expose evil*. St Paul exhorts us to ''Live as children of light . . . and find out what pleases the Lord. Have nothing to do with the fruitless deeds of darkness but rather expose them'' (Ephesians 5:8-10).

When Jeremiah was commissioned for his important prophetic task, the Lord said to him, ''Now, I have put my words in your mouth. See, today I appoint you over nations and kingdoms to uproot and tear down, to destroy and overthrow, to build and to plant'' (Jeremiah 1:9-10). There are four negative words and two positive. The work of the prophets of the Old Testament would have been totally ineffective if they had simply spelt out the right way without denouncing the evils of their day. John the Baptist continued in this tradition, and of course Jesus was scathing in his attacks on those religious leaders who led the people astray. He said very little about the Church which was to come, but he did make clear that discipline should be part of its life (Matthew 18:15–17). In the early days of the Church we have an awesome account of God's discipline of Ananias and Sapphira (Acts 5). St Paul, who wrote the best known and most beautiful poem on agape love (1 Corinthians 13), was constantly not only commending fellow workers, but denouncing false teachers or other ills. For example, in 2 Corinthians 11 he refers to "super apostles" who preach "a Jesus other than the Jesus we preached . . . a different spirit . . . a different gospel . . ." (v. 4) ". . . such men are false apostles, deceitful workmen, masquerading as apostles of Christ. And no wonder, for Satan himself masquerades as an angel of light. It is not surprising, then, if his servants masquerade as servants of righteousness" (vv. 13–15).

The issue of homosexuality

If evangelicals do not take a stand, or support those who take a stand, not only *for* the truth, but in a definite way *against* evil, then serious consequences follow. We have often found that the world understands this better than the Church. For example, over the issue of homosexuality, a leader in the *Daily Telegraph* in February 1990 stated, "Ordinary church-goers [and] the much wider public . . .still look to the national church for a lead in such matters'' (referring to the liberal Osborne Report, commissioned but not yet endorsed by the bishops). ''It makes no sense to assert, as the authors of the report do, that the scriptures and tradition of the Church are mere resources to be drawn on. They say that they should be free to interpret the Bible in the light of contemporary social conditions even though, as they acknowledge, there are no favourable references to homosexuality in it.'' (Remember that four out of seven members who produced the report were evangelicals.) ''The overwhelming view of the Bible and of Christian tradition is that extra-marital carnal relations, and all homosexual physical relationships, are sinful. . . . Religions such as Christianity are fundamentally revelation-based, or they are nothing. Each generation will, of course, bring its own understanding to that revelation; but there are certain central and timeless teachings that cannot be subject to passing intellectual fashions. People who doubt this would be much better off withdrawing from a church whose faith spans the best part of 2000 years.''

The Report records that only a third of bishops specifically called homosexual practice sin; some would knowingly ordain practising homosexuals or would ignore practising homosexuals if they were ''discreet''. The Bishop of Durham has said on television that he would not bar a practising homosexual from ordination. The (retired) Bishop of Birmingham, Hugh Montefiore, said he never asked ordinands about sexual activity, and did not want to know, as long as there was no scandal (interviewed on ''Kilroy'', February 1990).

Why is public pressure not put on such bishops by evangelical bishops to change their views or resign? Or have the evangelical bishops succumbed to the sort of views expressed in the Osborne Report? Either way Scripture is compromised. The end result of three decades of woolly thinking and practice in the Church of England over this matter is that we now have a scandalous situation on our hands. In one diocese alone, seventy of the clergy are said by the Lesbian and Gay Christian Movement to be active homosexuals. When Tony was researching the subject for the 1987 General Synod debate, the picture which emerged, including from letters written to him in confidence, was not only that of faithful homosexual couples living together in the Vicarage. As if that were not bad enough, it emerged there were also the men who changed from their clerical attire into their leathers to frequent the homosexual haunts. There was the letter from a mother distraught that her teenage son had been seduced by a group of homosexual clergy. Later there was the article in the *Church Times* of 23rd February 1990, about a homosexual clergyman co-habiting with one partner, who admitted he had received phone calls from another vicar who made forays into the big city and used to ask about "things unbecoming to a clergyman, places to go and so on". A letter in the same paper says that "Those who have been able to leave the gay scene – and to do that requires no small miracle . . . tell of the number of moves from one partner to another . . . Such a search results almost invariably in a downward spiral of self-indulgence . . . this search can often lead to liaisons with heterosexual teenage boys at a time in their lives when they naturally have great affection for members of their own sex. Introduced into a homosexual lifestyle, they are persuaded by homosexuals of their 'true' orientation. A few years later, however, the growth within them of what would have been a normal attraction to the opposite sex now serves only to confuse and torment, often with terrible results.''

What I believe has happened in the Church and the world over this issue as a result of the Church giving an uncertain sound, or even encouraging sin, is similar to what happened over the issue of abortion. The act legalising abortion in 1967 was ostensibly to remedy the squalor of ''back-street abortions''. Twenty years later over three million babies had been slaughtered. The Church was equivocating at the time the Act of Parliament was passed. Now church leaders, including some evangelicals, are being vague, or are actually positive about ''faithful'' homosexual practice even amongst the clergy. How will they monitor ''faithfulness''? By services of blessing – by a type of divorce procedure? The likely result is that bishops would turn a blind eye to anything other than scandal – in fact, that is the case now. And what advice do such clergy give to their church members and what example to non Christians? Only the scourge of AIDS is likely to prevent the end result in Church and nation being similar to that of the debauchery of ancient Rome.

Acceptance of false teachers continuing in office leads to acceptance of false teaching

Those evangelicals who have compromised either because of an unwillingness to expose the false teachers or because they are themselves becoming hazy over Scriptural truths in doctrine and ethics are only contributing to confusion and decline in Church and nation. The Church is suffering from such haziness in ways we could never have foreseen. The warden of an evangelical church community centre was asked two hypothetical questions by his left-wing local council. "Would you be prepared to allow a group of Muslims to be taught the Koran on your premises?" and "Would you allow a group of lesbians to have assertiveness training on your premises?" He answered "No" to both questions, but at first received no support at all in this stand from his evangelical bishop, even though it meant the threatened withdrawal by the council of a large annual grant for the excellent social work of the community centre. After pressure, the bishop then began to mediate between the two sides, believing that both were taking a "hard line". Hard line? What other sort of answer is an evangelical vicar meant to give to such questions? After further pressure the bishop became more positive in his support of the warden. When the synod of the diocese which includes this community centre discussed "partnership" with secular bodies and people of other faiths for inner city projects, an amendment was tabled that co-operation with such groups should be in "matters which do not compromise the distinctiveness of the Christian faith". This amendment was passed in a house of approximately 130 members by a majority of only three, with the evangelical bishop and some other evangelicals voting against it.

One of the questions posed to the Christian community centre is just a glimpse of problems the Church is facing over another major issue – the whole matter of interfaith relationships. If some evangelicals continue to compromise in matters of doctrine and morality they will be totally unprepared to face this greatest test. But first we need to examine the Charismatic scene to see if Christians in the Renewal movement are ready to stand firm for biblical truth and therefore combat deceit.

CHAPTER FOUR

Experience-centred Renewal

The house looked like an average semi-detached; nothing out of the ordinary, apart from the distinctive smell of incense which permeated every room. Tony and I were ushered into the livingroom, which was crowded with spiritualists. They had come to hear us speak, at the invitation of their leading medium, on the traditional teachings of Christianity. This had all come about because the local radio had heard that a group of Christians had staged a protest about two local events: the visit to Southend of the well-known medium, Doris Collins, closely followed by the New Age "Festival of Enlightenment", both held in the municipal "Cliffs Pavilion" on the seafront.

A group of leaders of different denominations had taken the initiative to call Christians together to pray, and plan any action. As a result, on the two occasions outside the Pavilion we distributed leaflets about the dangers of the occult and prayed that God would bring these events to nothing. On the occasion of Doris Collins' visit we specifically prayed for confusion, so that people would not hear clearly anything from the spirit world. We were delighted when a church member told us that one of her nonChristian friends, knowing nothing of our action, had confided her disappointment when she went to hear the medium, for people could not understand what Doris Collins was saying, to the extent that she became flustered and annoyed. Even more outstanding was the victory for Christianity following the so-called Festival of Enlightenment. After much intercessory prayer we petitioned the Council, pointing out the dangers of the occult and asking them not to allow such events on public property in future. Some of our church members were in the public gallery when the Council voted against accepting any future bookings from the Festival organisers.

Tony was invited on a local radio phone-in programme on the matter, when all kinds of people – Christians, agnostics, people into the occult and a local spiritualist medium – asked him questions. As a result we had the invitation to go to this local medium's home. We shared the possibility with the other leaders of our church for prayer, and with their support, accepted. We had the opportunity to share the Gospel without interruption for over half an hour. Some of the questions and discussion afterwards were rather heated. We obviously sensed a negative reaction when we talked about the Cross and stressed the Bible as the basis of our beliefs. One couple at the front sat perfectly still and silent till towards the end. We had noticed them particularly as they seemed to exude wealth and "presence". Towards the end of the discussion they asked in a seemingly casual way what the secret was of our success in banning the Festival of Enlightenment. Their conviction was that we must have had some influential friends on the Council or been able in some other way to pull strings. Tony and I both sensed the prompting of the Spirit to say very little about the prayer meetings we had held. It was only afterwards that our hostess informed us they were the nationwide organisers of the Festival. They must be high up in the world of the occult, which is well known for directing its own form of prayer against Christians.

The evening, from our point of view, had been a good opportunity for the Gospel. Just as we were thanking our hostess for her invitation, when everyone else had left, something happened which I found rather disturbing. There had been no opportunity for personal conversation with anyone else, but we wanted to assess the medium's reaction to the Gospel. We went over one or two points and asked for her comments. We were obviously used to all kinds of evangelistic situations and had dealt with anything from apathy to antagonism as well as more positive responses. But her reaction really distressed me. She actually gave us her "testimony" – of how she had been through traumatic situations in her life, but then she had met up with spiritualists and found not only comfort but "peace" with God and Christ. Her face shone as she spoke with obvious sincerity. It was extremely difficult to counter that – all we could do in the time we had was to point her back to the word of God which alone would reveal the deceit of spiritualism. That incident helped me to understand more of the strategy of Satan. He is majoring now on counterfeiting the *fruit* of the Spirit.

Counterfeit gifts of the Spirit

We had been aware ever since we entered into Renewal that the enemy could counterfeit the *gifts* of the Spirit. We used to be bombarded with stories about the satanic gift of tongues, such as the one (which to my knowledge

73

has never been corroborated) of someone speaking in tongues and a Chinese person recognising his own language, but pointing out that the tongues-speaker was uttering blasphemies. All this was intended to put us off Renewal. We decided that we would make our decision about the baptism of the Spirit and subsequent gifts on the basis of Scripture alone, and not experience, whether for or against. We reasoned that if there are counterfeit manifestations of the gifts, Satan would only trouble himself with them because he was worried about the current availability of the real thing. We have never witnessed a Satanic manifestation of that particular gift, though we have sometimes heard fleshly utterances, usually someone showing off their gift of tongues, the main use of which (unlike the rest of the gifts) is private, between the speaker and the Lord. We have, however, heard a Satanic counterfeit of prophecy and it was very obvious. With many of the spoken gifts, the flesh creeps in and it is hard sometimes to say what is really from the Lord and what from self. That is quite normal, and if handled correctly can be a learning process. But Satan often goes overboard and his activity can usually be easily distinguished from the Spirit, or even the flesh. In this case it was a young woman who either was not a genuine Christian in the first place, or who was a Christian but refused absolutely to listen to any advice. She therefore was not functioning as a member of the Body, but in dangerous isolation. She ended up uttering blood-curdling ''prophecies'' in a trance-like state and had, when all help was rejected, to be forbidden to do so.

I have also noticed counterfeit of the ability to distinguish spirits. In fact the whole realm of deliverance ministry is open to deceit. It is obviously true, as our Lord said, that Satan cannot cast out Satan (Matthew 12:26). But he can try to convince a Christian that there are demons present when there are not, and even counterfeit deliverance (of non-existent demons) to perplex and bewilder the troubled person and waste the time of counsellors. He can cause seeming demonic activity to erupt in one quarter, to distract us from his real work in another. I was present at meetings in a church where two women played havoc nearly every time the worship was taking off or the word of God preached. They would throw themselves down on the floor, or scream, or go into a trance. This had been going on for months. The minister and his wife, utterly sincere, greatly used by God in other ways and other situations, were convinced that if only they persevered in ministry to these women, the spirits would leave. In fact they told us that several had already been cast out, and it was only a matter of time before all the demons left. Hours and hours were spent in counselling and deliverance, whilst the congregation became frightened, bewildered or annoyed. The vicar tried to reassure them that God would be glorified in the end. My own discernment was that there was Satanic activity, but it was not in this case a matter of spirits afflicting the two women, but a demonic attempt to confuse the minister and distract the church, so that the work of God was hampered. If a firm line had been taken with the (subconsciously) attention-seeking women and the minister had called Satan's bluff, I am convinced the problem would have been resolved.

On the other hand we have found that the majority of people who make a profession of faith in Christ these days have had some dealings with the occult, from horoscopes to witchcraft, and need help. We encourage them to be detailed in their repentance of these things. Further counselling or deliverance is usually required if initially repentance has been inadequate, or the occult involvement very extensive. Some will have experienced counterfeit healing – perhaps through a spiritualist medium. The fact that "it works" must never be the sole criterion by which we judge a method. Yet many Christians would embrace certain very dubious forms of alternative medicine, because they cannot deny the good results. We have seen that the physical or emotional result may appear good, but spiritual deceit can so often take a deeper hold. In counselling, we would encourage a person to renounce the occult source of his healing before we pray for healing in the name of Jesus.

Unfortunately, some people, particularly Christian leaders, are so concerned about the possibility of counterfeit, that they run away from the real thing. This only serves to push thousands of people, desperate for healing, into the arms of Satan. If they cannot find counsel, healing and deliverance through their local church, we only have ourselves to blame if they turn to the occult.

Once the Holy Spirit has shown us the truth from his word about the availability of the gifts of the Spirit for the Christian today, then we live in disobedience if we do not eagerly desire those gifts (1 Corinthians 12:7, 31). We dare not make hesitation about using God's power, or fear of counterfeit, or of exercising discipline, our excuse. The Lord intended us to live in the realm of the Spirit and to exercise power for his glory, for the benefit of the Church and to help us reach out to unbelievers.

The enemy, in his "angel of light" guise, will obviously try every conceivable means to deceive, and will counterfeit every possible aspect of Christianity to confuse unbelievers and believers alike. His main aim is to prevent unbelievers from entering the kingdom, or when he fails with a person in that aim, to prevent that Christian from being effective in the kingdom of God, especially in winning others for Christ.

Counterfeit worship

Worship is something else which Satan can counterfeit. I know of two situations where this was the case. One of the older teenagers from our church decided to go to a "charismatic" meeting in London. Everyone was apparently worshipping in the way our friend was used to. They appeared to be open to the Spirit and lost in wonder, love and praise. However, he felt distinctly uneasy, so much so that he actually left the meeting. He thought there was something wrong with his spiritual life and discussed it with my husband. After a while Tony realised he had gone to a meeting run by a group about whom we had been warned. He had passed the warning on to our church but this teenager had not been present. These folk had started off well in the Christian life, but had given in to the flesh to the extent that the leaders' lives were riddled with immorality. As there was no willingness to repent, the enemy had a field-day in deceiving them and others. Praise God that the Holy Spirit had warned our teenage friend. We know of another church where the vicar had allowed the sort of situation we read about in 1 Corinthians to develop. There was chaos and licence, and although he did not approve of what was going on, he did not follow the very principles which St Paul spells out to bring order into such a situation. He could never understand why the gifts seemed to flourish and the worship appeared to be wonderful, yet he knew of the mess underneath. The enemy was of course working overtime to cause something, which had probably begun as a situation full of the potential of openness to the Spirit, to degenerate and become a vehicle for his own ends. The mess eventually erupted, swamped anything left that was good, and the church all but died. An even more disturbing example of the counterfeit is that New Age chanting can seem like worship to the undiscerning.

Counterfeit communities

The development of community life such as we read about in Acts 4:32–35 has often characterised the Renewal movement in one form or another. Once again Satan has his strategy for either infiltrating or counterfeiting this aspect of God's work. The extreme example of this is the mushrooming of hundreds of harmful cults, some of which might have a "charismatic appearance" at a superficial glance.

Counterfeit fruit of the Spirit

My assessment would be that, until the recent past, "charismatic counterfeits" have been fairly obvious. One has only had to dig a little to discover occult connections, or denial of the ethical or doctrinal teaching of scripture. Even if that was not obvious, the enemy, it seemed, held folk on a short leash. Healings were temporary and reverted, or "worked" physically but led to obvious emotional and spiritual distress. Leaders of cults appeared loving but were soon seen to be tyrants. But now that the "New Age", we are told, has dawned, Satan is working overtime to counterfeit the *fruit* of the Spirit. As his witting or unwitting agents work for the unity, peace and harmony of everyone and everything on planet Earth, so increasingly they are apparently characterised by love, joy and peace. Many New Age techniques such as transcendental meditation or yoga do bring a sense of well-being. I have seen people who radiate an inner glow which I would once have attributed only to a Christian. Behavioural patterns in the home or at work are affected positively.

This would not be such a dangerous ploy of the enemy if it were not that millions of Christians in Charismatic Renewal the world over have for years placed such emphasis on experience. That in itself does not invalidate a particular experience or mean that experience generally is unimportant in the life of a Christian. But it does mean that unless we are prepared to check everything by God's word, we could be in as much danger as those who deliberately devalue the Bible.

Christian experience

There is no denying that the *experience* we have of the Christian life is of vital significance. When God enters into covenant with a man, when eternal life is brought to birth in a human being, that is a work of Spirit to

79

spirit, of Being within being. Jesus said, "Flesh gives birth to flesh, but the Spirit gives birth to spirit. You should not be surprised at my saying 'You must be born again.' The wind blows wherever it pleases. You hear its sound, but you cannot tell where it comes from or where it is going. So it is with everyone born of the Spirit" (John 3:6-8). The life of the Spirit then grows and develops within us as we walk in the Spirit. But because we are human this hidden work will be made known to us, or manifested, in or through our bodies, our minds, our emotions, our wills, our senses. In other words, in our experience, in one way or another. It is true that there can be an inner "knowing" of the work of God in our lives which virtually bypasses the different processes connected with our physical being. "The Spirit himself testifies with our spirit that we are God's children" (Romans 8:16). But normally our bodies – with all their amazing complexity, including the working of the brain, the nervous system, the release of adrenalin into the system, etc. – are the vehicles through which we are made aware that God is at work. That is why St Paul urges us, "in view of God's mercy, to offer your bodies as living sacrifices, holy and pleasing to God – this is your spiritual act of worship. Do not conform any longer to the pattern of this world, but be transformed by the renewing of your mind. Then you will be able to test and approve what God's will is – his good, pleasing and perfect will" (Romans 12:1-2). It is vital that Christians continually follow Paul's advice about the dedication of minds and bodies to God so that what is *experienced* will be a *true* reflection of the eternal *hidden* work of the Holy Spirit, interacting with the innermost being of the children of God.

Incidentally, the fact that the body, taken as a whole, is the only vehicle for God to make known to a person his dealings within that individual, is the reason why sexual sin, although in one sense no worse than another sin, can have disastrous consequences for the spiritual life. Again, it is Paul who makes this point: "The body is not meant for sexual immorality, but for the Lord, and the Lord for the body. . . . Do you not know that your bodies are members of Christ himself? . . . he who unites himself with the Lord is one with him in spirit. Flee from sexual immorality. All other sins a man commits are outside his body, but he who sins sexually sins against his own body. Do you not know that your body is a temple of the Holy Spirit, who is in you, whom you have received from God? You are not your own; you were bought at a price. Therefore honour God with your body" (1 Corinthians 6:13–20). Satan recognises that if he can enslave people to sexual sin then he has control of far more than their bodies. Those Christian leaders who soft-pedal the teaching of the Bible on these matters, or even set a poor example themselves, have a lot to answer for.

Occult experience

With greater subtlety, Satan also knows that, because experience and feelings are so important to us in understanding what is happening to us spiritually, if he can cause men and women to "feel good", to feel healthy, to feel whole, then he has a strong hold over them. The Bible makes it clear that every human being is either in the kingdom of darkness, because of original sin which alienates us all from God, or in the kingdom of light, through repentance, and faith in God's Son. But in order to get an even deeper hold on people, Satan loves to see them enmeshed in any form of occult activity, including New Age techniques. The old-fashioned world of the occult was much more obviously evil. When the West was "Christianised" the majority abandoned paganism for at least nominal Christianity. Admittedly there was plenty of syncretism with superstition, but the deliberate choice by a minority to continue to dabble in the dark side of the occult, such as witchcraft, was regarded as abhorrent to the extent of being punishable by death. When the law against witchcraft was repealed in 1951, scarcely anyone could have foreseen that not only would there be an end to harmful witchhunts, but that the "craft" would be openly flaunted. It would be discussed on radio and television, and shown in a favourable light, including on serious documentary programmes, and witches would even be invited into schools to discuss their craft. Witchcraft became just another option to choose from amongst the varied array of alternative religions. The "black" side was played down, the "white" side promoted as positively useful to society. Even Satanism is being dressed up now to make it more palatable. We were sent a Satanist publication by an occultist who was trying to convince us that they no longer regard Christianity as a serious threat, nor do the majority of Satanists carry out blasphemous rituals, but rather the New Age is recognised as the milieu in which Satanism operates. The publication showed us that Lucifer is presented no longer as the epitome of all evil, to be worshipped by those who deliberately want to indulge in all forms of vile practices. Rather the propaganda now is that Satan, more often referred to as Lucifer, or even Pan, has been misrepresented by Christians and is worthy of worship. Not that we should be conned into thinking that the darker side is disappearing. The National Society for the Prevention of Cruelty to Children published a report in March 1990 in which deep concern was expressed by seven investigating teams about ritual abuse of children in bizarre or revolting Satanic practices. Satan will come out in his true colours every now and then, but mostly he will work overtime to appear "respectable".

This reversal of good and evil, making white appear black, and black white, is well described in a book about Findhorn, a major New Age community on the Moray Firth, Scotland. A man known as "Roc", Robert Ogilvie Crombie, has been very influential there. Although his experiences sound ridiculous, his influence, and that of Findhorn, should not be underestimated. Middle-ranking politicians have recently held a conference there to discuss the New Age, influential scientists go to Findhorn to study horticultural experiments conducted there, where amazing results are achieved through communing with nature, in the otherwise adverse climatic and soil conditions of Northwest Scotland.

Roc describes his many extraordinary experiences including one in the spring of 1966 in Edinburgh. "I had to cross what was known as the Meadows, a very wide green belt on the South side of Edinburgh Castle. . . . It was a beautiful evening, and there were few people about . . . then . . . I walked into an extraordinary 'atmosphere'. . . . This was accompanied by . . . heightened awareness and feeling of expectation. . . . Then I realised that I was not alone. A figure was walking beside me – a figure taller than myself. It was a faun radiating a tremendous sort of power . . . . *'Do you know who I am?'* I did at that moment . . . *'Then you ought to be afraid. Your word "panic" comes from the fear my presence causes.'* " Roc replied that he was not afraid "because of my feeling of affinity with your subjects, the earth spirits and the woodland creatures. *'Do you believe in my subjects?'* 'Yes' . . . *'DO YOU LOVE ME?'* 'Yes!' . . . *You know, of course, that I am the devil? You have just said that you love the devil . . .'* " Roc replied, "The Church turned all pagan gods and spirits into devils, fiends and imps . . . but it was wrong." ". . . Another encounter took place in September of the same year, 1966, at Attingham Park. . . . There was an acute feeling of being one with nature in a complete way as well as being one with the Divine, which produced great exultation. I was aware that he was walking by my side and of a strong bond between us. He stopped behind me and then walked into me so that we became one . . . I would stress the feeling of . . . intense exhilaration . . . peace, contentment, and a sense of spiritual presence . . . I am simply a channel he can use. . . . The main reason for this communication was the contribution it made to the work in the Findhorn Garden and its development . . . . It is important for the future of mankind that belief in the Nature Spirits and their god Pan is re-established . . . With such co-operation, what could be achieved would seem miraculous to many. It has been sought and asked for at Findhorn and the results have been given" (*The Magic of Findhorn*, by Paul Hawken, published by Fontana). The founders of the Findhorn community came to realise that in the end their main mission was not just to encourage harmony with nature and the spirit world behind it, but the transformation of the consciousness of man. Jesus is not shunned – in fact the adjective ''Christian'' is sometimes used to describe Findhorn (and we know of gullible Christians who have booked in for conferences there). But, to quote Paul Hawken's book again: ''Jesus is seen as a human embodiment of the Christ energy, not somebody nailed to the cross. In other words, he is a joyous messenger of God, a person who embodies and signifies transformation. Pain and suffering are absent from the Findhorn theology.''

I used to wonder how it would be that when the antichrist came, so many millions would want to worship him, for hitherto only a tiny minority in this world have ever deliberately and knowingly worshipped Satan. Now, in our own time and in our own nation, there are increasing numbers of seemingly normal, often professional people who have been totally deceived into worshipping the devil/Lucifer/Pan, believing him to be working for the good of humanity. The supreme blasphemy is that this is even said to be in co-operation with Jesus. There are thousands more throughout the world influenced by communities such as Findhorn, unaware of the connection with the devil in the background.

The Christian answer

Christians, apart from the very gullible, are probably confident that they could discern and overcome such deception. Jesus has won the victory, he triumphed over sin, death and the devil 2000 years ago, and we are taught that by *faith* we can enter into that victory in the spiritual battles we have to fight today. But do we understand that true faith comes by believing and acting on God's *word*? In the examples of deceit and counterfeit which I have cited, those problems would not have arisen if biblical principles had been followed. For example, we need the release of God's power through the gifts of the Spirit, such as those described in 1 Corinthians, but we also need to maintain the discipline and order of church life which St Paul stresses in the same chapter. If we allow chaos, licence, immorality, then obviously we give a foothold to the enemy who can begin to infiltrate or even take over. If we use the gift of discernment or any other, it needs to be checked out by those Christians who are more mature. Independence or isolation are very dangerous in the Christian life. Holiness of life and the continual offering of the mind, body, will and emotions back to God are essential. Again and again, we come back to the teaching of Scripture, which underlines just how dangerous it is to deny, neglect or water down any aspect of the Bible, or to be unbalanced in over-stressing one major aspect of truth to the detriment of another. Yet I believe the Renewal movement is facing just such a danger.

Vulnerability in the Renewal movement

In overemphasizing the importance of beneficial experience, Charismatic renewal is now particularly vulnerable at a time when the enemy is counterfeiting the fruit and gifts of the Spirit. Since writing that sentence, I have been to a conference at Holy Trinity, Brompton, London, at which John Wimber introduced "the Kansas City Prophets" to several hundred Christian leaders. It is not part of my purpose to comment on that controversial ministry. But what distressed Tony and myself was, that despite strong pleas from a tiny minority of leaders, including the two of us, there was no attempt, in fact there was even resistance to the idea, of first checking out this ministry with Scripture, and allowing plenty of time for assessment before it was launched on the Christian public in the UK in October 1990. Almost to a man, it seemed, well-known charismatic leaders were caught up in the excitement of hearing Paul Cain's accurate words of knowledge. The fact that there could be no human explanation for his amazing gift was enough for the majority there to endorse this ministry. This, despite the fact that only two weeks prior to the London conference, there had to be a public confession of their glaring errors. Time will reveal what is of God, and what is not. Unfortunately much of the Christian public is not allowing that time. If our only criterion is "it works and seems beneficial", then heaven help the renewal movement.

It is possible to turn Christianity on its head in our longing to "deliver the goods". While not in any sense wanting to denigrate the vital ministry of healing, I sometimes wonder if it has not become the "be all and end all" of the gospel message. Of course we must preach and practise it. Our own church is a healing community, and hundreds of people have found spiritual, emotional and physical healing within it through the power of Jesus. The longing of my heart is that this ministry will be even more powerful as needs abound, and in the context of the burgeoning of the occult. Human beings must be treated as whole people to be loved, not just "souls on legs" to be evangelised. If men and women are suffering or in need, if they are living in circumstances of deprivation and degradation, if they are oppressed by injustice or possessed by the enemy, then Christians must be there at their point of need, just as Jesus was, with the same compassion and the same power, whether or not folk respond to him. For the last two centuries Christians have been at the forefront of social change for the better, and long may that continue.

Yet in their concern that Christians should not be so heavenly-minded that they are no earthly use, the opposite can be the result. Whether it is concern for social justice or being involved in a counselling and healing ministry, these excellent causes can become ends in themselves. In our search for wholeness, we can forget brokenness before God. In our longing for healing we can forget a theology of suffering. What was it Paul Hawken wrote? "Pain and suffering are absent from the Findhorn theology." Yet what of Charismatic theology? If the blessings of turning to Christ are emphasised out of all proportion, it can only end in the Christian Church jostling for position with other religious or occult groups as we peddle our wares. If in some cases better results seem to be achieved, for example in healing, by another method, then the sufferer will move on to the next market-stall. Christians themselves may be tempted to succumb to deceit because of the over-emphasis on healing. A Christian sister in a hospice told me of the powerful temptation she sensed when nursing a personal friend who was dying of cancer. Although experts in pain control, the medical staff were unable to succeed in this particular case, where the pain affected the nerve ends. Yet they knew of case histories where a particular occult form of alternative medicine had been effective. It was only with great difficulty that my friend was able to resist the temptation to turn to this method, when orthodox medicine and prayer seemed to no avail. I wonder how many Christians would stand firm in such a situation, watching a loved one die in agony?

Not only does the over-emphasis on healing and other benefits make us vulnerable when God does not appear to answer positively, but I believe it also results in self-centred Christians.

Although I have benefited from and been used in "counselling", and we have a counselling department in our church, because we believe that Jesus wants to heal emotions and personality defects as well as bodies, yet I react against those ministries which encourage Christians to go for *regular* counselling. I have heard it described as peeling the layers of an onion. The problem with that is there is nothing left at the end. There are times and situations where further counselling is appropriate, but the grave danger is of encouraging Christians to be turned in on themselves, always concerned lest there is a further hangup or even demon which needs to be dealt with.

I sometimes think I preferred it when Christians were happy to put up with some eccentricities but got on with putting into practice the basic principles of repentance, and dying to sin and self, being crucified with Christ, rather than constantly searching for "wholeness". "Wholeness" is, I believe, a result of (though it should not be the motive for) dying to self. Jesus said, "If anyone would come after me, he must deny himself and take up his cross and follow me. For whoever wants to save his life will lose it, but whoever loses his life for me and the Gospel will save it" (Mark 8:34,35).

The world and large sections of the Church will, in the days to come, be happy to embrace the "Jesus" who is a "joyous messenger", "the embodiment of Christ energy", (according to Paul Hawken) but reject the true Jesus, who was nailed to the Cross and who expects us to be "crucified with Christ" (Galatians 2:20). I firmly believe that in revival God will do a work in the lives of those Christians who hunger and thirst for righteousness, which will show us all over again how to be a Good Friday people so that we can more truly become an Easter people.

I believe our message to unbelievers must also change in emphasis. We should encourage people to worship God for himself, because he is God and there is no other. If we continue to sell Christianity for its benefits alone I believe God could *allow* us to be outdone by the enemy. He wants to restore worship of himself for his own sake, he wants to reinstate a holy awe, even a right fear of the One who has ultimate power over our eternal destiny. In revival I believe men and women will cry out to be right with God because of who he is, on the basis of what his Son did on the Cross; they will want peace with God not because they have been told what a wonderful *experience* peace is, but because of an understanding that true peace is a state of being restored to a right relationship with God. If feelings follow, that is up to God. They will understand that love is not necessarily a wonderful feeling but a total self-giving to God

90

and man. But what of joy? Perhaps in revival God will usher us into that state of being, where whatever we have to endure from the world, the flesh and the devil, we can still lift our faces up to our Lord and Saviour without grumbling or complaining.

When the emphasis in the life and preaching of Christians is God-ward, based on his word, then I believe that as a side effect, and unsought, we shall have the *experience* of love, joy and peace in far greater measure than ever we do when we seek it. With that balance in our lives and message, we need not fear the powerful deceit of the New Age or anything beyond that, which the devil has planned. We need not fear turning to the left or right at the crossroads. Because Jesus has defeated death, the enemy is completely powerless when faced with self which has been crucified. When that is our testimony, when we follow the way of the cross, we shall know resurrection, we shall be in revival. But first, we must negotiate another major hazard – the increasing trend towards interfaith compromise.

CHAPTER FIVE

Parting of the Ways

"How many of you here tonight were Hindus or Buddhists before you were converted to Christianity?" I was addressing a meeting in Singapore, where earlier in the day we had glimpsed something of the many temples of different religions in the thriving, modern city. About half the people that evening raised their hands in response to my question. I knew that for many of them their step of faith would have meant a traumatic break from the beliefs and traditions of their families. Yet because of the relative freedom of religion in Singapore, compared with many countries, most of the Christians, who account for nearly twenty per cent of the population, experience little in the way of persecution. They are a missionary-minded church, and know what it is to support the spread of the Gospel, including in nearby countries where it can be a matter of risking one's life to evangelise or become a Christian.

In such a setting it came as a shock to a group of clergy when we told them that in the UK some of us are beginning to experience opposition, not from un-believers but from other churchgoers, for upholding the uniqueness of Jesus as the only Saviour, and for resisting interfaith compromise.

I know of a believer in Israel who has been at risk from the Muslim Brotherhood ever since he converted from Islam to Christianity. Yet despite the danger to his life he witnesses fearlessly about his faith. I wonder how he would react if he were to learn that the Anglican bishop in Jerusalem (Bishop Kafity) has stated that his responsibility is to dialogue with people of other faiths, not convert them, because he believes Christ is to be found already in Judaism and Islam.

I wonder about the reaction of tens of thousands of people throughout the world, who have suffered as a result of turning from other religions to a living faith in Christ, when they discover that in many countries there is an orchestrated campaign to bring people of the major faiths together, not only to dialogue but to worship. I wonder how Anglican missionaries felt, some of whom have sacrificed career, possessions, family, and even risked health or life itself to spread the Gospel, including to people of other faiths, when they learned that Dr Runcie, as the Archbishop of Canterbury, made speeches which were scarcely an encouragement to their endeavours, to say the least.

In a lecture at Lambeth palace in 1986 on "Christianity and World Religions", Dr Runcie said that we should "recognize that other faiths than our own are genuine mansions of the Spirit with many rooms to be discovered, rather than solitary fortresses to be attacked. . . . All the centuries that the Spirit of God has been working in Christians, he must also have been working in Hindus, Buddhists, Muslims and others. . . . We must learn to recognize the work of the Spirit at the centre of each of our faiths." Before he went to India "there were the certainties of an encapsulated Western Christianity; after, there are new ways of thinking about God, Christ and the world. . . .

Encounter with other faiths can deepen and enrich us . . . there is a certain incompleteness in each of our traditions . . . ultimately all religions possess a provisional, interim character as ways and signs to help us in our pilgrimage to Ultimate Truth and Perfection. . . . We will have to abandon any narrowly conceived Christian apologetic, based on a sense of superiority and an exclusive claim to truth."

This was a recurring theme for Dr Runcie which he reiterated at the Global Forum of Spiritual and Parliamentary Leaders on Human Survival in April 1988. "We must . . . recognize the 'divine spark' in all human beings. . . . and that the unity of all human beings is grounded and crowned in an ultimate unity which is greater than the recognition of it in each of our traditions." It would be unfair not to point out that Dr Runcie did in both speeches use phrases about the uniqueness of Christ and said, "For my part, I am bound to say as a Christian that definitive apprehension of the divine occurs in an encounter with Jesus Christ". Many Christians would be reassured by the latter statement and fail to understand that, given the context of syncretism, the key words are "For my part". In other words the revelation of God in Jesus is unique for *Christians*. Isn't that rather a truism?

Universalism

The problem with universalism ("we all get to heaven in the end") is that it is so attractive and compelling. All Christians are encouraged to nurture the fruit of the Spirit in their lives, including patience, kindness and goodness. Consequently the biblical teaching that "man is destined to die once, and after that to face judgement" (Hebrews 9:27) can seem extremely unpalatable, for it seems to imply there is a cut-off point to the patience, kindness and goodness of God. If only it were not true about heaven and hell. If only Jesus were not the *only* way to the Father, or that at least the nonChristian attains eternal life through Jesus without realising it. Such thoughts are bound to bombard our minds.

The pressure of agonising over such matters leads vast numbers of Christians to concede either in principle or in practice over the more exclusive biblical teaching. They either ignore the relevant teaching or relegate it to superstition of an earlier age. Even numerous Christians who still retain a theoretical belief in Jesus as the only Saviour from the coming judgement, do very little about the teaching in practice, being less than fervent in the rescue mission of evangelism. We seem to have a blockage over any heart belief that people without Christ really do go to a lost eternity. Once again, we turn Christian truth on its head, looking at it through the spectacles of human sympathy, which cause everything to appear topsy-turvy.

The only way

We need to ask God for his wisdom, for insight into his way of looking at things. If we really believe in a God who considered it necessary to send his eternal Son into this world to be born, to suffer, to die and rise again for us – how can there be any other way? What kind of a God would do that if there were any way to avoid it, knowing that inherent in becoming human was the grave risk of the Son of God falling to temptation, and therefore sin? The alternative for Jesus was to take the path of sacrifice, which ultimately led to the Cross, which was his purpose in coming into the world. Clearly one can choose not to believe in Christianity at all, but once the choice has been made to place one's eternal destiny in the hands of the God revealed in Christ, then bound up in that decision is the conviction that for a God of love and justice, there was no other way. In the words of the old hymn: "There was no other good enough, to pay the price of sin; He only could unlock the gate of heaven and let us in." Only the God-man could bridge the gap, and only by the Cross. In my imagination I picture the angels waiting, scarcely daring to breathe, to see if the plan of salvation would be carried out to the end. When Jesus cried out on the Cross "It is finished!", the uncomprehending disciples wept in grief; the crowd mocked, but the angels must have rejoiced in exultation, and the Father wept tears of joy. The Godhead had taken the ultimate risk, which could have led to disintegration (possibly of the universe itself), but the end result was victory over sin, death and hell.

Never in the history of the world had there been such a demonstration of pure love, that God, in the second person of the Trinity, died for mankind. Then came the mighty miracle of the resurrection, the great commission, and after the ascension the empowering of the disciples to take the story of salvation to the ends of the earth. As we have seen, in his wisdom the Holy Spirit of truth saw to it that the story of "the Word [who] was with God, [who] was God . . . [who] became flesh" (John 1:1,14) was spread abroad not just by word of mouth but in written form. But once an individual hears the word about God's Word, a life-changing decision must be made in this life. "God did not send his Son into the world to condemn the world but to save the world through him. Whoever believes in him is not condemned, but whoever does not believe stands condemned already because he has not believed in the name of God's one and only Son" (John 3:17,18). This is the sticking point, yet it is inherent in God's redemption and revelation. When the almighty God makes known to a man that he has acted in such a risky, unnecessary and glorious way on his behalf, a response is essential and inevitable. If that response is negative, whether through neglect or rejection, that is in effect to despise the death of God, made necessary by our sin; to despise the only way back to a restored relationship, made possible by that death. Just as God cannot be unloving or he would be untrue to himself, so he cannot, as a holy God, be unjust and ignore the rejection of the divine plan of salvation. It would make a mockery, to say the least, of all human justice, which must be derived from the divine attribute.

For justice and judgement to make any sense there will be differences, not only in the major distinction between a man spending eternity with God or being separated from him according to his decision in this life, but differences also within those two states. (Hence the stress in the Bible on rewards and punishment.) There is obviously also justice for those who have never heard, but at this point I believe we should leave suspension marks. Human beings will insist on carrying things to a logical conclusion, whereas my firm and previously stated conviction is that all great truth is to be found in paradox. If we seek to resolve it by trying to cause two parallel lines of argument to merge, we are seeking to achieve the impossible, and it will result in disastrous heresy.

Therefore I believe that trusting to the love, justice and mercy of God, the only course of action open to every Christian is to "go and tell" (according to our different gifts and circumstances). Many of us fail in this through fear, apathy or lack of encouragement from the Church. Praise God for the continuing possibility of repentance and forgiveness. He understands our weaknesses. That is a different matter from abandoning any attempt at evangelism because of a mistaken belief that in the end God will accept everyone. Becoming more common is a humanly adjusted Gospel shared in dialogue rather than proclamation. I am convinced that any such compromise of the message, any watering down, can only result in conveying the message of a salvation-plan and, ultimately, a god which are products of imagination, not revelation. For anyone to worship such a man-made god is to break the first commandment of all. This god who accepts everyone in the end, perhaps after numerous life-cycles or purgatory or some other form of chance after this life; this god who sent a christ who is not the Christ, to be an example, not a sacrifice; to be *a* way, not *the* way; who apparently permeates other religions – such a god, worshipped and proclaimed by numerous churchgoers including many of our religious leaders, is *not* the God of the Bible.

The choice before us is as always – the way of the cross as revealed in Scripture, or the broad way of our own making. God is not a man that we can ignore him, belittle him, despise him, reduce him to our understanding, or make his character and his ways a matter of opinion and conjecture. He has acted, he has spoken, he has made the only way of salvation perfectly clear. Those who lead others astray on these matters, particularly church leaders who should know better, can only be heading for extremely severe judgement.

The interfaith movement

Every Christian will be forced to choose in the near future whether to follow the way of revelation or that of imagination, as pressure is brought to bear upon the whole Church from the interfaith movement. It is now closely connected with the New Age movement, and in fact is an aspect of it from the point of view of enemy strategy, although this would not necessarily be recognised by all those involved.

I remember the day when Tony and I stumbled on recent serious developments in the orchestrated campaign for interfaith worship, although, as previously stated, there has been interest in interfaith dialogue for about a hundred years. It was in March 1989. Five years before that we had founded Action for Biblical Witness to Our Nation. We believe that God guided us to mention three main issues in the original letter which we sent to all the 11,000 clergy in the Church of England in 1984. As we raised the matters of doctrinal concern, exemplified in the Durham controversy over the virgin birth and empty tomb; ethical issues, particularly homosexual practice in the church; and the whole matter of interfaith compromise, we did not realise at the time that God was actually setting us an agenda for action. A Christian leader with a prophetic ministry approached us when Tony was going to put forward his private member's motion on moral issues to the General Synod in 1987. He asked us to consider seriously taking up the grave matter of the previous Archbiship's interfaith speech in 1986, which I have quoted. Both of us knew that although an important issue, it was not God's time to take up the interfaith matter. We followed the advice in Exodus 23 about seeking to advance little by little. This was just as well, for we could not have foreseen the massive media attention which was to dominate our lives for several months surrounding the General Synod debate on homosexuality.

In March 1989 we were in the middle of leading a houseparty for another church, but made time to visit an ABWON supporter who had something of interest to share with us. She had in the course of her professional work heard about and attended services in cathedrals which stressed harmony between people of all faiths. Our friend had been horrified at what she had experienced, and even more as she researched the background to the liturgies used.

Tony and I both had a sense that this was God's time for us to act on the interfaith matter. We had vaguely heard about these events in cathedrals, but as the evangelical reaction appeared to be a deafening silence, we had naïvely thought that perhaps the situation was not so serious. The conversation with our friend changed all that. As with the setting up of ABWON in the first place, there were three major ways in which the Holy Spirit confirmed to us the rightness of the timing and our involvement. In both cases Tony and I heard and responded to God's call in faith. The first confirmation was that shortly afterwards there was a major development in the Church of England which was obviously what God had been preparing us to confront. Secondly, at the same time on both occasions, in 1984 and 1989, we suffered very much from the action of close friends – experiences which can be far more damaging or debilitating than the more obvious attacks of the enemy. Yet in a back-handed way any such opposition is confirmation of being on the right track. Thirdly, we prayed about every aspect with our local church and would not have moved ahead if God had not confirmed through them that it was the right timing and the right action.

The Canterbury Festival

The development in the Church of England which was brought to our attention in 1989 was the Canterbury Festival of Faith and the Environment. A brochure about it came through the post in the Spring of that year. Tony and I react to developments in very different ways. I normally have an immediate reaction of "prophetic discernment", whereas Tony responds much more slowly, preferring to find out as many facts as possible. Each is an important corrective to the other, combined with the further necessary insight of the local Body of Christ.

As I read the brochure I felt a sense of deep grief. At the heart of the Anglican Communion, which incorporates 52 million people worldwide and influences millions more, there was to be an interfaith event. In mockery of the ancient pilgrimages to the Cathedral, the brochure stated: "Now new pilgrims will be coming: up to 150 people drawn from many faiths and from environmental organisations will make their way along three routes to Canterbury, where their arrival on the afternoon of Friday 15th September will herald the official launch of the Festival." The first pilgrimage was to be led by an Anglican clergyman, the second by a Baha'i, and the third, starting at the Hindu temple near Watford, was organised by Ranchor Das, a Hindu devotee and member of the International Consultancy on Religion, Education and Culture (ICOREC), religious advisers to WWF (World Wide Fund for Nature), which has been working with the major faiths for some years on environmental issues.

In this way it can be seen how those with concern for the environment, who quite naturally want co-operation from the major faiths, can be used in promoting interfaith events, which readily lead to interfaith worship, so compromising Christianity. The brochure went on to explain that "All day on Saturday 16th September the Cathedral will open its doors and grounds to the largest celebration ever of religion and ecology. All the faiths and environmental organisations of the UK are invited to use the space for exhibitions . . . or whatever other medium they may choose to express their concern for nature."

The reason I was so certain that this was the occasion about which God wanted us to begin in a major way to protest against interfaith and New Age issues, was because I had several months earlier had an opportunity to speak a prophetic word in Canterbury Cathedral itself.

I had been attending an international Charismatic

103

Leaders' Conference in 1988, the climax of which was to be a celebration in Canterbury Cathedral. The theme was holiness, unity and evangelism. We were informed that the context would not be appropriate for an open time of ministry including the gifts of the Spirit, but anyone who believed that God had given a prophetic word for the occasion should share it beforehand with one of the organisers, who would assess whether it was appropriate. It so happened that during one of the more informal gatherings I sensed that the Lord wanted to speak through me in the gift of prophecy, but there had been no obvious opportunity. I wrote it down that night, not knowing there would be any chance to share it, but aware that it had an importance beyond my human understanding, which should not be lost. Consequently I felt I had little choice but to offer to read it out in the Cathedral, even though I was extremely nervous at the prospect. Having been granted permission, it seemed the service was developing in such a way that the opportunity would pass. It is difficult to describe the sense of urgency which I had to ensure this was not the case. This was particularly so as during the service I believe the Holy Spirit prompted me to add one sentence to what I had already written down, to do with the Cathedral itself. At last I was beckoned to the lectern. My nervousness vanished, but I read the following with heavy heart:

> My dear ones, I have been speaking to you of holiness. And indeed it is the longing of my heart that you should be like me, that your heart should beat with my heart, that you should know what it is to love as I love. But I would warn you of my enemy who comes as an angel of light, to deceive you with counterfeit love, with human

sympathy rather than divine compassion. For the time
is coming and now is, when I would have you love and
praise me for my kindness and sternness, for my
miracles of judgement as well as deliverance. For it is
through them that many will turn to me, and so you
must love as I love, for my Son is Judge as well as
Saviour. I have been speaking to you of unity. And yes,
you are beginning to understand that you must reflect
my divine nature in its harmony. But I would say to
you I am a God of creativity. The unity which I long to
see amongst my children will be a diamond with many
facets. Each facet will reflect something of my
revelation but is of little worth unless part of the whole.
So there must be a glad recognition that you belong
together and need each other. But again I would warn
you, my children, that my enemy is seeking to bring
about a unity which is not based on my word. It will
appear to have as its goal the peace of this world, but it
is not centred on the cross of my Son. I am warning you
of these things for I would not have any of you deceived
by wandering down the path of acceptance, leading to
toleration of any form of worship which does not
uphold my name and my word. The end of that path is
that many will one day worship a christ who is not my
Son. *The very stones of this building will witness this terrible
thing, unless my church repents.* And now my children, I
call you to give yourselves to the task of reaching the
world with my Gospel with a new sense of urgency in
your hearts. For the days are dark, the time is short.
But how will you reach this world? By following the way
of my Son who died and rose again. And so I would
have you die to yourselves, die to your reputations.
Above all I would have you lead those I have entrusted
to your care in the way of costly discipleship. For too
long some of you have emphasized the comfort of my
Spirit and not his power. Now you are learning
something of his power, but would you use that only for

105

the healing of one another and not to witness to the lost? *I have called you to care for my people in order to prepare them for costly sacrifice. Some who prefer cosy comfort will turn back, but I commission you to make true disciples, for it is only through them that the world will see the risen glory of my Son.*

The words in italics were those I was prompted to add in the Cathedral. When the brochure about the Canterbury Festival was sent to us the following year, I knew in my spirit that when worship which was not centred on Jesus took place at the Festival, that would be the *beginning* of the fulfilment of the words that there would be worship one day in Canterbury Cathedral of ''a christ who is not my Son''.

It was hard to know what action to take over the Festival as we were to be abroad in New Zealand and Israel for the best part of two months, arriving back on the Friday the Festival began. In the end we wrote to the three thousand people (half of whom are clergy) on our ABWON mailing list, alerting them about the event, and to participants of the Canterbury Charismatic Conference reminding them of the prophecy. We urged prayer primarily, but also letters of protest to the Archbishop and Dean of Canterbury. We encouraged folk to join in the Nationwide March for Jesus which happened to be on the same day as the Festival, but suggested that a few join us on the Saturday for peaceful distribution of evangelistic leaflets, which also warned people about the interfaith and New Age elements.

God answered prayer about the event in definite ways. First of all when a member of our congregation telephoned the organisers for details, the lady answering the phone volunteered the information that important changes had been made because of the protests. We know that Dr Runcie and the Dean were swamped by letters about it, and we think that as a result the Cloister Events were moved from the Cathedral cloister to the grounds of the adjoining Christ Church College. Those events were a complete flop – far from being "the largest celebration ever of religion and ecology" hardly anyone turned up in the daytime on Saturday. I stress that we are not against co-operation over ecological matters, but against the New Age elements and interfaith worship.

The cathedral authorities denied that there had been any interfaith worship. Yet a group from our church, in a peaceful demonstration of protest, who followed the interfaith procession on the Friday to the gates of the Cathedral and were allowed up to the door, obtained a copy of the liturgy used by the pilgrims. Although the liturgy included some biblical material from Psalms and Proverbs, there was no mention of Jesus at all. Candles from the multi-faith pilgrimages were actually used to light the paschal candle, representing the light and wounds of Christ, making a mockery of its symbolism. There is no possible description for that service other than "interfaith worship". On the Saturday night I attended "The Celebration of the Forest", which the organisers were at pains to stress was not a worship service. Nevertheless, I found it a disturbing experience to listen to a Buddhist salvation story about a Monkey King (which was not even balanced out by a biblical story) read out in the crypt of the Mother Church of England. A school choir sang in the nave words representing the beliefs of Brazil's Yanomami Indians: "The trees have power. We worship them. We live because they give us life.'' The programme I was given actually stated that the song was written by composers who had also penned songs about the Witches of Pendle Hill. Evidently this was thought to be a commendation, despite the problems clergy in Lancashire have to face, dealing with oppression, possession and the aftermath of blasphemous rituals as a result of the activities of Pendle witches.

The hardest part for me personally at Canterbury was to see the way my husband was treated. My reaction was not because of personal hurt – we should rejoice when opposed for Christ's sake. Although the ''persecution'' was absolutely nothing compared with that faced by many Christians through the centuries and elsewhere in the world today, it was its significance which grieved me deeply. As we had only returned from Israel the previous day, Tony had decided to distribute leaflets with supporters during the day on Saturday, and I just went to the evening event. I arrived as it was beginning to grow dark. The magnificent Cathedral was towering above me, illuminated against the evening sky, but it was not long before the atmosphere was marred for me. As people of seven faiths queued to go in, I watched cathedral security guards steer Tony, an Anglican rector and member of General Synod, out of the gate. This was apparently the third time in the day that they had done this, on orders from the Dean, who incidentally had been a personal friend some twenty-five years ago at college. All this because the ABWON supporters peacefully distributed Christian leaflets, which the Dean had decided to ban, and sang songs of worship in the grounds, out of earshot of anything else going on. Yet Hindus were allowed to meditate, and Buddhists distribute recruiting leaflets for children. These were all welcomed. But a man who had been in the Church of England ministry for twenty-two years, who has been instrumental in hundreds of people becoming Christians and growing in the faith, who has encouraged men into the Anglican ministry, and others to stay when they wanted to quit – he was asked to leave the grounds of Canterbury Cathedral. I sensed the Lord's grief for the consequences which will result if the Church of England continues down this road. Jesus has much to say about religious leaders who strain out a gnat but swallow a camel. A Christian leaflet was banned, but occult literature was welcomed. Bishops are appointed who lead people astray, clergy are allowed to be practising homosexuals, or are re-appointed after committing adultery and remarrying, or even in some cases after scandals involving abuse of children. Interfaith worship is encouraged, confusing thousands, yet those who speak out against such things have become victims of the steamroller of the liberal establishment.

God's judgement can be the only result for any church which no longer upholds the biblical teaching about the Cross and Great Commission. We should take careful note of the words of Archbishop Cranmer, who wrote: "If the Church proceed futher to make any new articles of faith beside the Scripture, or direct not the form of life according to the same; then it is not the pillar of truth, nor the Church of Christ, but the synagogue of Satan and the temple of antichrist."

People have said: "Surely the appointment of George Carey is a sign of God's mercy, not his judgement?" Certainly I believe he will encourage the

Church of England to make the most of the Decade of Evangelism. If he also leads us in a return to biblical principles, there could be major reforms as a result. But despite many signs of life especially at parish level, the fact remains that there is much compromise, much that is rotten, at the heart of the system.

New Age/Interfaith events in Cathedrals

The enemy appears to have launched a campaign to infiltrate the Church of England through using its cathedrals. Cathedrals were often built on the intersection of ley-lines – supposed avenues of supernatural occult power – on sites originally occupied by pagan shrines. The idea was to reclaim these places for the true God. However, it is possible that if Jesus is not always glorified by what goes on in cathedrals or churches, occult forces can return. We have certainly known of ancient parish churches where this was the case. When the World Wide Fund for Nature, with doubtless entirely worthy motives, chose to harness the major religions of the world to promote concern for the environment, its religious advisers decided to use English cathedrals for this purpose. From their point of view that was a brainwave. But from the point of view of the purity of Christianity it has been a disaster. Whether cathedral authorities are gullible, deceived or actively co-operating in seeking to bring in New Age and interfaith concepts, is open to question. What is certain is that, with the willing co-operation of deans, the most extraordinary events have been taking place in our cathedrals. At a similar event in Winchester Cathedral, members of other faiths were welcomed as "brothers and sisters in faith". Everyone was invited to use "as sources of prayer, inspiration and reflection", readings from Bahai'sm, Buddhism, Hinduism, Islam, Sikhism and Taoism. During this service all the participants of many faiths made "a covenant between us and our neighbour; between us and God; between us and nature. It is designed to be made by all those of good will, of any religion or none." This was called the Rainbow Covenant. The rainbow has unfortunately been adopted by New Agers as their supreme symbol of seven psychic rays. The Covenant was sealed by each participant tying a rainbow-coloured thread on his neighbour's wrist. This is based upon the Hindu practice by which earth energies are channelled from women to men. Over a thousand churches across Britain and the world used the service simultaneously that day, and a thousand in Britain since then. Nine million tuned into a related meditation on the BBC World Service. One only needs a little spiritual insight to recognise how rapidly deception is spreading.

The strong Hindu influence was also to be found in the Creation Festival Liturgy staged in Coventry Cathedral by WWF in October 1988. It included a prayer: "Our brothers and sisters of the creation, the mighty trees, the broad oceans, the air, the earth, the creatures of creation, forgive us and reconcile us to you." In the context of the worldwide pervasion of Hinduism, this cannot be seen as merely poetic language. Millions of Westerners are embracing Hinduism, many of them without realising it. For cathedrals to use such language is dangerously misleading and damaging. A WWF bulletin (*The New Road*, Issue No.5) commends "humanity collaborating *with* Nature. To get to that stage is going to involve a very profound journey of change within human beings. It will require a 'death' to the way we have hitherto understood ourselves and our relationship with Nature . . . a journey from 'mastery' to 'mystery'. . . . The central issue is recognition of indelible mystery as the start of the new stage in the age-long journey.''

The Canterbury event was meant to be the greatest of these creation festivals held in British cathedrals. It was not until afterwards that we realised what God had accomplished through prayer. He had at least temporarily stemmed the polluted tide of interfaith/New Age teaching and practice which was being welcomed into our cathedrals, and from them influencing churches throughout our country and beyond. At a Creation Festival in Salisbury Cathedral in the Spring of 1990 the organiser, the Rt Rev. John Bickersteth, stated that the festival ''was not multifaith, unlike three previous controversial Creation Festivals. . . .'' He said that while he had personally valued sharing The Peace (in the Communion Service) with two Buddhist monks at Canterbury last autumn, the interfaith nature of the event had made ''many devout churchmen wary of engaging at all in this supremely biblical theme'' (from an article in the *Church of England Newspaper*). Of course we were castigated as unthinking fundamentalists, as against the Green Movement and even as racists, none of which is true. According to the *Guardian* of September 18th 1989, ''Mr Jonathon Porritt, director of Friends of the Earth, said the protest was 'profoundly unecological. One of the first principles of ecology is diversity. These fundamentalists have nothing whatsoever to offer either humankind or the planet.' He said

112

many Anglicans were keen to see the Church doing more on environmental issues, 'but they need to know they're not going to be walloped by the fundamentalists.' '' According to Dr Habgood, ''the attacks were a most distressing example of closed minds''.

If Christians, who are concerned that the biblical teaching of Jesus as the only Saviour should not be lost, are prepared for such criticism and opposition, then there is hope that the stemming of the tide will not just be temporary. In ABWON we have asked supporters to join ''Cathedral Watch'', to keep an eye open for interfaith events planned for cathedrals (or churches), with a view to possible further protest. If there is not massive, determined prayer and action in the power of the Spirit, we shall be like King Canute. Without a doubt the Church of England, and the Anglican church in some other countries, will be swamped by a tidal wave of interfaith compromise. This will spread to other denominations and have far-reaching implications for the nations concerned. It also underlines how vital it is for Christians to overcome any temptation to compromise through any weakened view of Scripture or human sympathy. We need to check every experience against the teaching of Scripture. It may be extra-biblical, but it should not be unbiblical.

We often admire the views of the evangelical theologian, Dr P. Forster of St John's, Durham University, but we were saddened when he wrote in the *Church Times* about his view of cautious acceptance of interfaith celebrations, allowing various religions slots for their contribution. He believes there is room ''for an imaginative ambiguity in the language and imagery

. . . provided this does not result in a deliberate fudge of issues''. He cites the annual Commonwealth Day service held in Westminster Abbey in the presence of the Queen, as a positive example. Yet when Tony attended this event in 1990 to discover the facts, he found the experience anything but innocuous. There were readings from a Hindu text focusing on Brahma, the Hindu creator-god, and from the Koran extolling the virtues of Allah. There were prayers and praise to the Buddha ''dear to gods and men – who brings the truth'', to Brahma, to Allah whom ''alone we worship'', and to God the true Guru who is ''everything and in everyone''. The name of Jesus was mentioned only at the end of two prayers. Somehow I cannot imagine any of the apostles or early disciples finding a rationale for such a service. Yet many evangelicals could be influenced by Dr Forster's views. In ABWON we launched a petition to the Queen about this service.

Where will it all lead? Jesus told a compelling story about ten virgins who went to meet the bridegroom, but only five were ready when the bridegroom arrived. ''The rest became drowsy and fell asleep. . . . the virgins who were ready went with him to the wedding banquet. And the door was shut. Later the others came. 'Sir! Sir!', they said. 'Open the door for us!' But he replied, 'I tell you the truth, I don't know you' '' (Matthew 25:5, 10–12). Jesus also said in Matthew 7:21: ''Not everyone who says to me, 'Lord, Lord,' will enter the kingdom of heaven, but only he who does the will of my Father who is in heaven''; and in Matthew 24:11–13: ''Many false prophets will appear and deceive many people. Because of the increase of wickedness, the love of most will grow cold, but he who stands firm to the end will be saved.''

It is clear from this teaching that there is a true church within the nominal church. There are apparently many who believe themselves to be followers of Christ who will prove not to be, for various reasons. No one should be complacent, and certainly we shall not see the true picture until the next life. Throughout history some Christians have become so distressed by what they have seen as unbiblical development in a major branch of the Church that they have opted out and formed a ''purer'' denomination. Then that has become corrupt and so history repeats itself. Nevertheless, I believe that we are given a glimpse, particularly in the book of Revelation, into a scene of major apostasy in the Last Days. We are told there will be a worldwide religion inspired by ''the dragon'' (Satan) who will give ''the beast his power and his throne and great authority''. This may well refer to the powerful human being referred to elsewhere in the New Testament as the man of lawlessness or antichrist. ''The whole world was astonished and followed the beast . . . All the inhabitants of the earth will worship the beast – all whose names have not been written in the book of life belonging to the Lamb that was slain from the creation of the world'' (Revelation 13:2,3,8).

The prospect of a worldwide religion which is anti-Christ no longer seems so remote – and as nominal Christians are not in the Lamb's book of life they will be involved with it. Christians who compromise will obviously be in a position of great danger. I foresee a situation where major ''Christian'' denominations which become involved in interfaith and New Age compromise, or churches which are entirely experience-centred, will drift and gradually merge into this world religion, failing to notice that they have begun to worship a different christ. Only true Christians who are alert will escape the deceit of those days, for the enemy is working overtime to deceive church people. The decisions we make now about our attitude to God's judgement in this life and the next, to interfaith worship and to the New Age, could well determine whether we drift into a worldwide apostate church, or are amongst those who will be ready for Jesus when he comes again.

CHAPTER SIX

God and the Nations

I began to understand much more about how the Church and nation in the West came to be in such a serious predicament, when I was in Greece in 1989. We were on holiday as a family, partly as a treat for our children celebrating their 18th and 21st birthdays that year. Everything was perfect. The sun shone every day and the combination of coast, countryside, Greek hospitality and the opportunity to explore ancient sites, both biblical and classical, was idyllic. One afternoon we explored Korinthos. As I was walking away from the centre of the old city of Corinth towards its main gate, along the broad road paved with Roman stones, gleaming white columns on either side, I paused to take in the beauty of the scene. The classical lines of the town, the imposing hill of Acrocorinth behind me, the blue bay spread out below, spring flowers in abundance in the fields around. "Well, Paul had some perks", I thought. Somehow as a child I always imagined the towns described in my Sunday school lessons about St Paul as being a maze of dingy, murky streets – the association in my mind I suppose with mob violence, lashings, imprisonment and every other form of persecution endured by the great man.

The next day we devoted to exploring the Parthenon and surrounding sites. One of the seven wonders of the world, it must have dominated the Athens of Paul's day. He too would have marvelled at the brilliant engineering which ensured that the Acropolis formed a suitable foundation for this amazing edifice, brainchild of the genius Pericles, master architect in the fifth century BC. Built of beautiful white stone, glistening with a gold hue in the sunlight, each slender pillar was deliberately constructed slightly out of true, creating an illusion of perfect symmetry. Although dedicated to the goddess Athena, it was never more than a shrine, as even Pericles' contemporaries recognised its uniqueness and used another temple for regular worship.

By contrast the little hill called the Areopagus, where the Senate used to meet, is insignificant. Yet it was here that a profound truth was to be revealed to the respected philosophers of Athens, a truth which was to change the nation. Classical Greece rose to such heights in philosophy, political thought and art that its influence has remained with us ever since. Students today still debate who were the true conquerors – the Romans with their military might which dominated the world of Paul's day, or the Greeks whose brilliance in other realms captivated the hearts of the Romans. Whether Paul was impressed or not we shall never know. All we do know is that when he stood on the Aeropagus in AD 54 at the invitation of the Senate, to explain what they regarded as a new philosophy, he was deeply distressed because ''the city was full of idols'' (Acts 17:16). He had been trying to find out as much as possible about the religious views of the Athenians. It is food for thought that despite the heights they had achieved in other areas of life, the Greeks only had a strange pantheon interwoven with extraordinary legend, to whom they directed their worship. To escape, some branched out into deeper forms of philosophy whilst still retaining their idols. Others went the way of even more unthinking superstition, to consult the oracle at Delphi, where a deranged priestess sat in eerie darkness. Her incoherent mutterings, as interpreted by a devotee, would determine the course of human events, from marriages to wars.

Some Athenians, searching in their spirits for something more, had through the general revelation available to all men, been able to sense the existence of a God who was different from all other gods. They had built an altar with the mysterious inscription "TO AN UNKNOWN GOD".

Now was to be their unique moment of special revelation. The true God, the only God, was about to make himself known to the Athenian intelligentsia, through his servant Paul. In the famous words of Acts 17:23 Paul declared, "Now what you worship as something unknown I am going to proclaim to you." Nearly two thousand years later we stood at the foot of the same hill, gazing at the plaque inscribed with the words from Acts 17, marvelling that, beginning with Dionysius, the first convert from the Senate, Christianity spread, so that still today 97 per cent of Greeks are nominally Christian.

But it was not until I was relaxing on the deck of a boat cruising around the Greek islands, that suddenly so much seemed to fall into place. Lest anyone thinks that I am super-spiritual I just want to say that my human preference would have been to think about nothing in particular as I enjoyed the sun and the sea. It has always been a mystery to me that my more profound thoughts rarely come to me in times set aside for prayer. God often surprises me at the most inconvenient times, in this case as our family sat in deckchairs in a little corner of a rather crowded boat.

Looking back I realise that subconsciously something had been bothering me as we travelled around Greece. Previously I had only been to Holland, Germany, Israel and New Zealand. It was the first time I had seen with my own eyes in concrete (or rather stone) reality such an abundance of remains of another world, another culture, another religion. Actual encounter is so very different from history lessons. In my imagination I tried to enter into the daily lives of the Greeks of long ago, including the religious observances woven into their culture. These people knew no other way. They had no concept even of monotheism and no one to tell them – *or had they?*

I felt compelled on that boat to look up again in my pocket Bible the account of Paul's time in Athens in Acts 17. Here was something of an answer – a ray of hope: "In the past God overlooked such ignorance" (v. 30). The other side of the coin is to be found in Romans 1:20: "For since the creation of the world God's invisible qualities – his eternal power and divine nature – have been clearly seen, being understood from what has been made, so that men are without excuse." We can only dimly perceive from these two statements that for those who were seeking the truth there was the possibility of discovering something of the eternal, almighty, invisible and only God through his work in creation. But that same God knew that it was only by special revelation that more about him could be known. In the mystery of his purposes he chose just one man called Abraham, and the obscure nation descended from him, to be the objects of that revelation. The intention was that they would share with the rest of humanity the knowledge of the One who revealed himself to Moses as "I am who I am".

Sadly, few heard of these profound truths. If they rejected God's general revelation in creation there was little hope. If they continued to seek then there is a hint of God's mercy and justice in Acts 17:30. But all was to revolve around God's master plan. The ultimate truth about God was to be revealed in the person of his Son, living, dying on a cross on a little hill, and rising again.

And now, here was his apostle, Paul, on another little hill, declaring these truths to philosophers. The Areopagus symbolised the heights to which human thought could soar. Calvary showed us that "the foolishness of God is wiser than man's wisdom, and the weakness of God is stronger than man's strength" (1 Corinthians 1:25). "Jews demand miraculous signs and Greeks look for wisdom, but we preach Christ crucified: a stumbling block to Jews and foolishness to Gentiles, but to those whom God has called, both Jews and Greeks, Christ the power of God and the wisdom of God" (1 Corinthians 1:22-24).

As, on the boat trip, I read Paul's sermon to the Athenians, two words seemed to stand out: they were "NOW" and "NATION". Deep in my spirit, I sensed just something of the way God has chosen in his sovereignty to work out his purposes, not only for individuals but also for nations*.

Ultimately, of course, God will reveal his Lordship

* Readers may like to turn to the summary of my argument, at the end of this chapter, before reading on.

over the whole of the universe. It is self-evident that God – the very definition of all that the word sums up: "I am who I am", the essence of existence and being; "Yahweh", Lord, Sovereign One – will one day be seen to be God over the whole of creation (all that exists and has existed) and over all subsidiary lordship: all kings, princes, rulers, governments; and all that is governed: every nation, tribe, language and people.

In God's unfathomable wisdom, confounding the wisdom of the world, he chose a lowly human birth, a criminal's death, the subsequent actual moment of resurrection unseen by man, as the way of triumphing over sin, death, hell and every power that would oppose the ultimate revelation of his sovereignty. But he also had his time to reveal that to each nation in turn.

God's "Now" time for nations

As part of his plan God has his "NOW" time for each NATION. In Acts 17:26,27 we read: "From one man he made every nation of men, that they should inhabit the whole earth; and he determined the times set for them and the exact places where they should live. God did this *so that* men would seek him and perhaps reach out for him and find him, though he is not far from each one of us."

It is obvious that the life of each one of us is bound up in what happens to our nation. As for eternal matters, although it is as individuals that we shall stand before God, and meanwhile the Holy Spirit has a tailor-made way of dealing with each of us, yet for the majority that is bound up with God's dealings with our nation.

122

A different time of revelation for each nation

When we read in Acts 17:30 that "in the past God overlooked such ignorance [i.e. their idolatry] but NOW he commands all people everywhere to repent", it is also obvious that the "NOW time" is different for each nation. For the Athenians (and soon most of Greece) it was there and then. As Paul said, "NOW what you worship as something unknown I am going to proclaim to you. The God who made the world and everything in it is the Lord of heaven and earth" (Acts 17:23,24).

Although God can reveal himself supernaturally to men, by and large he has chosen to use the preaching of the word as his instrument, for "How can they hear without someone preaching to them?" (Romans 10:14). God's "NOW" time for revealing the Gospel to each nation and tribe was, and still is, dependent on believers fulfilling the Great Commission, although speeded up first by the printing press then by modern media, communications and transport. The borders and duration of nations obviously vary, but even those factors are determined by God (Deuteronomy 32:8, Acts 17:26). It is certainly in his plan as to how and when the Gospel is taken to a nation. Rarely is anything in God's dealings with man neat and tidy, according to our assessment. There are many instances where missionaries went to distant lands and at first made little impact. But I could now see that God has an overall strategy and timing to make his revelation in Jesus Christ known in a major way to each country. His "NOW" time is different for each nation. The communication of the revelation is second only in importance to the act of salvation itself. Prior to that, men are in the same state of ignorance as the Athenians before Paul preached to them, and we can only trust their eternal destiny to the mercy and justice of God.

The time of God's revelation to a nation is, of necessity, epoch-making in its significance. We can only appreciate this if first of all we are gripped by the astounding nature of God's revelation in Christ. As we read in the first chapter of John's gospel, it was the Word who was in the beginning wth God, who was God, through whom all things were made, in whom was life and light, who came into the world. This one who came from heaven had to be lifted up (on the Cross) "that everyone who believes in him may have eternal life" (John 3:15). We Christians become so accustomed to these truths that we cease to wonder at the implication of this for the Godhead and for mankind.

God deals with nations as a whole

We also need to be convinced that God does deal with nations as a whole and not just with individuals. In the NIV Complete Concordance one can count that the word "nations" is used 553 times in the Bible, 294 of which are in a context where the word "world" would be equally appropriate. This is an indication of the importance given through divine inspiration to the division of the world into separate nations. We have already noted God's sovereignty over the boundaries of nations in Deuteronomy 32:8: "When the Most High gave the nations their inheritance, when he divided all mankind, he set up boundaries for the peoples according to the number of the sons of God" (NIV margin).

124

The disciples are commissioned by Jesus to "Go and make disciples of all nations" (Matthew 28:19). We are encouraged to learn in Revelation 5:9 that Jesus, with his blood "purchased men for God from every tribe and language and people and nation". This is confirmed in Revelation 7:9, and in chapter 14:6,7 we discover that an angel has been appointed to oversee the task of proclaiming the eternal Gospel to every nation. His message is: "Fear God and give him glory, because the hour of his judgement has come. Worship him."

God's mercy and judgement are not just for individuals but for nations. Key verses here are to be found in Jeremiah 18:7-10: "If at any time I announce that a nation or kingdom is to be uprooted, torn down and destroyed, and if that nation I warned repents of its evil, then I will relent and not inflict on it the disaster I had planned. And if at another time I announce that a nation or kingdom is to be built up and planted, and if it does evil in my sight and does not obey me, then I will reconsider the good I had intended to do for it." History teaches us of the rise and fall of many nations and kingdoms. We live in an epoch-making time as the mighty USSR sways and totters, some say soon to crumble and fall. Events are happening so fast that Sally Brompton wrote in *The Times* at the end of 1989: "A British lecturer in political science who has been contracted by the Oxford University Press to write a book on communist systems of the world, is refusing to sign the contract on the grounds that his subject matter is fast disappearing. 'I have suggested that if there is nothing left for him to write about he could do a book on the collapse of communism instead', says Henry Hardy, OUP's political editor."

Who could have imagined a short time ago that the seemingly impregnable Iron Curtain would be torn open with the breach of the Berlin Wall, that communism would collapse in one country after another in Eastern Europe, nationalistic uprisings then threatening the USSR itself? Whose hand but that of almighty God could have brought about the convergence of a number of significant events? If they had come singly then each one might have been overcome, but together they proved too much, even for the mighty Soviet Union. The strident Soviet voice against Star Wars made it obvious to the world that the necessity to keep up with such technology was too much for a Russian economy far too top-heavy in its defence expenditure. Chernobyl horrified the Soviet Union mainly because of its economic implications. Still today whole villages wait to be evacuated at enormous expense, huge areas as large as England and Wales to the north of Chernobyl cannot be farmed for who knows how many decades to come, health has to be continually monitored in over 700 villages, and technology of nuclear power stations revised. President Gorbachev, meanwhile, was emerging as a man not only with a charismatic personality, but with the courage to embark on *glasnost* and *perestroika*. This combination of factors amongst others was to ignite the flame required for the seething cauldron of discontent to boil over.

God, it seems, had allowed a little over seventy years for the rise and humiliation fo the world's first totally atheistic empire. We ignore his warnings at our peril.

We have noted that the distinctiveness of nations appears to be important in Scripture, that God is sovereign over their boundaries, rise and fall; that God

126

has his main time for the Gospel to be taken to each nation, and that there will be Christians from every nation. We are also given a glimpse into the future and we read that the nations will be judged. "When the Son of Man comes in his glory, and all the angels with him, he will sit on his throne in heavenly glory. All the nations will be gathered before him and he will separate the people one from another." The criteria for determining judgement or blessing concern the extent to which justice and mercy were shown to those in need.

Is Israel significant in God's purpose for nations?

A more controversial criterion for the judgement of nations is found in Joel 3:1-3: "In those days and at that time, when I restore the fortunes of Judah and Jerusalem, I will gather all nations and bring them down to the valley of Jehoshaphat. There I will enter into judgement against them concerning my inheritance, my people Israel, for they scattered my people among the nations and divided up my land." Many Christians who take these scriptures seriously, but see no significance in the purposes of God for the modern state of Israel, interpret prophecies referring to Judah, Jerusalem, Isreal, etc., as having sole reference now to the Church. This is known as Replacement Theology. Christians usually feel very strongly about their particular viewpoint. Replacement theology does have far-reaching consequences, affecting not just one's view of present day Israel but of God's purposes for the Last Days. I personally find the biblical evidence alone quite overwhelming in supporting the literal reading of Israel as the primary reference. But that has been so well argued by others that it might be more helpful as we consider God and the nations to approach the subject another way. In so doing we must not lose sight of the vital truth that nations will also be judged according to their reaction to Christianity and the Church. This I believe to be the dual reference of these prophecies. However, many details make no sense at all if the literal Israel is not referred to.

If we accept that God is sovereign over nations, then the modern state of Israel cannot be an exception. One could debate whether it is only in his permissive rather than purposive will. If we, for the moment, accept such a simplistic distinction, and that it was not God's plan "A" for Israel to be re-established, where I wonder did God intend those escaping from the holocaust to find a home, safe from anti-semitism? And now that thousands of Jewish people are being allowed to emigrate from not only Eastern Europe but also the USSR, and even the USA is placing severe restrictions on their immigration, should we not be thankful that they have their own state to go to?

At the time of writing, in a "World at One" Radio 4 programme, figures were given of as many as 4,000 immigrants a week arriving at Tel Aviv, alarmed by a new tide of anti-semitism. The atmosphere in the USSR is dangerous, threats have been made against Jewish people, who are being used as scapegoats. Russians are not ready yet to take responsibility for their terrible history of the last seventy years. Central power is weaker, Jewish people are being allowed out and possibly a million more will go to Israel. Some would see their plight as little different from that of the Boat People, but surely we must make a distinction between refugees fleeing from their own country, and a distinct people seeking refuge in what was once their land, and has now been re-established. The question of the treatment of Palestinians must remain another, though obviously important, issue, beyond the scope of this book.

If we once admit the hand of God in the establishment of modern Israel, at least as an act of mercy to suffering Jews, isn't it rather too much of a coincidence that there are so many prophecies in the Old Testament, and some in the New, which if taken as having a primary reference to the literal Israel, fit present day events exactly? So in Isaiah 11:11,12 we read in the context of a prophecy about the Messiah coming to rule the earth, "In that day the Lord will reach out his hand a second time to reclaim the remnant that is left of his people . . . he will assemble the scattered people of Judah from the four quarters of the earth." St Paul prophesies in Romans 11:25,26: "I do not want you to be ignorant of this mystery, brothers, so that you may not be conceited: Israel has experienced a hardening in part until the full number of the Gentiles has come in. And so all Israel will be saved." Sanday and Headlam, in the *International Critical Commentary*, commenting on "all Israel" say, "The whole context shows clearly that it is the actual Israel of history that is referred to. . . . It cannot be interpreted either of spiritual Israel, as by Calvin, or the remnant according to the election of grace, or such Jews as believe, or all who to the end of the world shall turn unto the Lord . . . [all] must be taken in the proper meaning of the word: Israel as a whole, Israel as a nation, and not as necessarily including every individual Israelite."

I can understand people finding this idea a stumbling block, especially when they consider the agnosticism of the majority of early Zionists and the many blunders and even atrocities committed by Israeli Jews against Arabs, even allowing for the obvious anti-semitic bias of much reporting. (One example of this bias was the contrast between the world outcry against the Israeli invasion of Lebanon and the whimper when the Syrians invaded a few years later.)

So often I think Christians miss the main point about the significance of Israel in God's purposes. One can understand divergent views about prophecy, when it would appear just as easy for God to fulfil promises about the restoration of Jewish people to himself when they are scattered all over the world, as when many (and it may still remain a minority) are gathered in one country which had been inhabited by all kinds of people for centuries. But the matter takes on a whole new perspective when we consider God and his dealings with the nations. If God one day will establish his sovereignty over the nations of the world, would this not be undermined if the land which he had promised to his original chosen people (recorded for us 160 times in the Old Testament) belonged to others? Fifteen of these 160 promises state that the land is to be theirs ''for ever''. Although the promises are conditional on obedience, there is nevertheless always the promise of restoration to the land (recorded twenty-four times in the Old Testament). If, as will surely be the case, the Jewish people keep their country (give or take some changes in boundaries) then an amazing scenario of fulfilled prophecy becomes possible. Jewish people, including in Israel, are turning in ever increasing numbers to the

Messiah. In Zechariah 12 we read that Jerusalem will be attacked by all nations, but the attack will fail through divine intervention. Then the Lord pours out his Spirit on the people of Jerusalem and "they will look on me, the one they have pierced" (v. 10). In Ezekiel 39, after a similar description of a massive attack, we read in vv. 25-29, "I will show myself holy through them in the sight of many nations."

The divine purpose in the restoration of Jewish people to the land of Israel is only partly to facilitate their recognition of Jesus as the Messiah. In itself that could have been accomplished in other ways. I believe it is mainly so that God can once more establish a theocracy in the only country where he was ever truly recognised as King, and that only intermittently. This will be such a miracle that it will have an effect on all the nations of the world. It is not so much that other nations will be Christianised, as that in some way as yet beyond our comprehension, they will recognise the only true God in the Person of his Son as ruler of the world, and bow the knee, even if in fear. "As you have been an object of cursing among the nations, O Judah and Israel, so will I save you, and you will be a blessing . . . And many peoples and powerful nations will come to Jerusalem to seek the Lord Almighty and to entreat him" (Zechariah 8:13,22).

For Jesus ultimately to be seen as victorious he, who has always been despised and rejected by men, will reveal his sovereignty over, and destroy, "all dominion, authority and power. For he *must* reign until he has put all his enemies under his feet" (1 Corinthians 15:24,25).

Now that we have glimpsed something of God's

dealings with the nations in the Last Days, history takes on a new perspective. It is often described as "His Story" and part of that story is God's timing for the Gospel to be taken to nation after nation.

An over-view of God's dealings with nations

As I write I have in front of me a map of the Roman Empire after Christ – its boundaries, sea routes, land trade routes and main roads. God certainly knew the right time to choose for the initial spread of the Gospel. It is possible that a handful of missionaries took the message (without making major impact) as far as India and even China. That is where the world's main ancient civilisations and empires arose outside of the earliest in Mesopotamia and Egypt (other than smaller, later civilisations in the Americas). An interesting fact is that at its height the Roman Empire had a population equivalent to that of Britain today (in excess of fifty million) which was also the population of China in the first century AD, according to the *Times Atlas of Ancient Civilisation*. The task facing the disciples as a result of the Great Commission was only a fraction of what would have been the case if Jesus had not come until much later.

Christianity soon became established in the Middle East and Europe. What was to become Orthodox Christianity spread through what is now Eastern Europe and further East. Who could have foreseen in those amazing early years, when Christianity spread like wildfire, that soon the divinity of Jesus would be denied in country after country where some of the earliest churches had been established, as Islam advanced, demanding submission to the will of Allah.

132

It was not long before Christianity made a deep and abiding impact on our own country. Our laws were to be based on it, our culture transformed by it. God had chosen to use Britain not because there was anything special about us, but because we could be an instrument to spread his Gospel. A sea-going nation, we would one day have an empire on which the sun would never set. Unfortunate mistakes were made by some missionaries, mixing true Christian values with colonial attitudes. For some aspects we should hang our heads in shame, for others we knew no better. Even so, many thousands throughout the world, in the USA, Canada, Australia, New Zealand, Africa and many other places, came to a true knowledge of Jesus Christ.

The link with revival

God's "NOW time" was arriving for nation after nation. In the early days of British missionary endeavour, in order to ensure that teaching more true to the word of God would be proclaimed, the Holy Spirit brought about a nationwide revival, probably the greatest we have known. This was the Wesleyan revival in the eighteenth century which transformed our country for fifty years or more.

Sometimes when Christianity was taken to another country it was a rather secondhand version. I believe that revivals were often either sent by God for a major purpose, as with the Wesleyan revival, which may have saved our country from the equivalent of the French Revolution, and promoted the spread of the Gospel abroad, or elsewhere they were the first truly indigenous expression of that country's Christianity.

Some of the revivals in Africa fall into that category.

The last few decades seem to be God's "NOW time" for the Far East. As missionaries were expelled from China, so many went to countries scarcely touched by the Gospel. Often the word "revival" is used incorrectly, when what is really taking place is a tribe or even a country eagerly responding to the Gospel for the first time ever. In other cases it may not be the first time missionaries have visited a country, but it is the time the Holy Spirit has chosen for the Gospel to make a major impact on that land. The mushrooming of churches in South Korea, including Yoido Full Gospel Church in Seoul with over half a million members, or the amazing stories we hear of between fifty and a hundred million Chinese becoming Christians in the most adverse and unlikely circumstances, are examples of this. This does carry the implication that when Christian leaders point to revival taking place all over the world, and go on to make the assumption, as I used to, that God will not leave out Europe, it is a misunderstanding of what is actually happening. *I believe it can be an unwitting insult to the justice of God to expect him to deal in the same way with nations which have had their main time of revelation and largely turned their back on it, as with nations or tribes discovering Jesus for the first time.* It also means that men like Paul Yonggi Cho, pastor of the fastest-growing church in the world, will usually be disappointed when they teach certain church growth principles in the West, expecting similar results.

Two implications of God's "NOW time" for nations

It was this sweeping view of God's purposes for the nations, his plan to allow each nation its "NOW time", which I understood in a moment on that boat as we cruised round the Greek islands, not far from the cradle of Christianity. Although details were filled out in my thinking later, I saw immediately two major implications of the outworking of God's purposes in history. One I have already referred to: very often "revivals" are not really that at all, but rather the first major impact of the Gospel on a country or tribe. In other cases there may be genuine revivals but often there is a specific reason for them. For example, Britain experienced a number of revivals because of its key role in the spread of the Gospel.

Secondly I saw just how vital God's "NOW time" is in the history of each nation. This is the opportunity for thousands or even millions of people to learn about the astounding revelation of God in Jesus Christ. Their response is vital, not only on a personal level but for the future course of that nation. In some countries it deeply affects the government and the country's laws (although any liaison of Church with state will have disadvantages), or it is a movement amongst the people, acting rather like yeast in dough.

Serious consequences for a nation turning its back on God's revelation

As this time of revelation for a nation is so vital I also saw that it follows that it is a *deeply serious matter* when a nation begins to turn its back on that revelation. We have seen that only too vividly in the USSR. What then of the UK and other Western countries? Many believers are sensing something of the grief in the heart of God as they realise the extent of our rebellion against him.

We were a pagan nation, but were increasingly affected by Christianity from the third century onwards. "By the third quarter of the seventh century a generation of churchmen emerged who combined the order and authority of Rome with the emotional and imaginative vigour of Celtic Christianity. Aidan of Lindisfarne, the first Celtic churchman to take an active part in the mission to the Anglo-Saxons, with a number of other Anglo-Saxon churchmen, such as Wilfred of York, took the lead in overcoming paganism and racism. . . . The Synod of Whitby in 664 confirmed the Romanization of British Christianity" (*Lion Handbook: The History of Christianity*). We still had to go through the superstition of the Middle Ages. Then came the Reformation, and Protestant Christianity, with the occasional setback, was to flower for centuries, boosted later by our main revival – the Weleyan and subsequent continuing Evangelical Revival. But the seeds of doubt sown by rationalism in the seventeenth century were nurtured by deism in the eighteenth century, to come to the full flower of scepticism, Darwinism, humanism, Freudianism, and, in the Church, liberalism, in the nineteenth century. Two world wars later, with materialism and hedonism flourishing, we were ripe as a nation to begin to revert to paganism – manifested in pantheism, animism, Druidism, and many other "isms", even Satanism itself.

In Romans 1:18 we learn that "the wrath of God is being revealed from heaven against all the godlessness and wickedness of men, who *suppress* the truth by their wickedness." Even more worrying is Matthew 12:43-45: "When an evil spirit comes out of a man, it goes through arid places seeking rest and does not find it. Then it says, 'I will return to the house I left'. When it arrives, it finds the house unoccupied, swept clean and put in order. Then it goes and takes with it seven other spirits more wicked than itself, and they go and live there. And the final condition of that man is worse than the first. *That is how it will be with this wicked generation.*" I must confess that I had never previously noticed the corporate reference in that verse and had always thought of it as referring to an individual, as obviously it does as well (Luke 11:24-26). However, as we learn elsewhere that there are rulers, authorities and powers over this dark world and spiritual forces of evil in the heavenly realms (Ephesians 6:12), so it would seem that whereas they can be driven away from a generation of people (presumably in a certain area or nation), equally they can be allowed back in greater force.

I believe that is our present state as a nation. I believe God's hand of protection was lifted from us in the 1960s, and we have fallen prey to terrible forces of the evil one. We have even put out a welcome mat for gods "new" and old. Each evil indulged in results in our becoming slaves to the power manipulating that evil.

To summarise: I saw on my holiday in Greece, that God had planned his time to reveal the Gospel to each nation, in a major way. What is often confused as revival is in fact God's NOW time for that nation, or has some other special significance. Furthermore there are bound to be extremely serious consequences for a nation which largely turns its back on Christianity. We cannot expect God, in his justice, to deal with such a nation in the same way as one which is experiencing the full power of the Gospel for the first time. Scripture shows that God deals with nations as a whole, including through judgement.

Although part of the Church in the UK may still be purified by revival and many thousands of unbelievers rescued as a result, I remain unconvinced that as a *nation* we shall experience God's mercy. It is so important that we do not become false prophets predicting "Peace, peace," where there is no peace.

CHAPTER SEVEN

Prophecy and the Last Days?

"First of all, you must understand that in the last days scoffers will come, scoffing and following their own evil desires. They will say, 'Where is this "coming" he promised? Ever since our fathers died, everything goes on as it has since the beginning of creation' " (2 Peter 3:3-4).

Eschatology – the doctrine of "the last things" such as the Last Days, the Tribulation, the Second Coming, death, judgement, heaven and hell – is low on the agenda of most preachers and teachers. Reaction against the old-fashioned hell-fire and damnation preaching has been almost total in the West. There was a time not so long ago when pre-millennial teaching was popularised once more in the States, and books on the subject were eagerly read in the UK. This is the view that Jesus "raptures" the saints to heaven before the Great Tribulation and his return to a literal one-thousand-year reign on earth. Pseudo newspapers were published as if to report the staggering event of millions of Christians vanishing from the earth in "the Rapture". Certain predictions were made related to current events, but they did not come true. Confusion reigned. Some reacted with cynicism. Others, such as those who were to become leaders of the various strands of the Housechurch Movement in England, met together to discuss their understanding of eschatology. They emerged with a triumphalist view of God's kingdom being restored here and now, in other words, ushering in the Millennium before the return of Christ.

Liberal theologians have always dismissed this sort of teaching. Any discussions about pre-millennial versus post-millennial views would be regarded by them as totally irrelevant in any case, because they would even reject straightforward teaching on the Second Coming as inconceivable.

On the other extreme, fundamentalists disagree so much over different views that the average evangelical seeks to avoid such controversy by making as little reference to eschatological matters as possible. If he is honest with himself, he believes in eternal life and some sort of heaven, is rather uncomfortable about referring to hell, and teaches that Jesus will come again in the future. If an Anglican, he declares this in the Creed Sunday by Sunday, and knows that he should enthuse his congregation about it at Advent, but really thinks it will not be in his lifetime. Perhaps he is rather sceptical about any teaching to do with signs of the End Times. The last thing the average evangelical preacher wants to do is to stray into the territory of future prophecy, lest he be proved wrong.

New Testament emphasis on eschatology

Yet this attitude is so very different from that of the writers of the New Testament. Perhaps we do not normally think of St Peter, the impulsive, lovable disciple, as a prophet. Yet I have quoted only a little from the last chapter we have of his writings – in fact almost the whole chapter contains specific teaching on "the day of the Lord" and the destruction of the heavens and the earth. It is noteworthy that at the beginning of his very first sermon at Pentecost he immediately sets his powerful message about Jesus of Nazareth in the context of eschatology, quoting the famous passage from Joel 2. We are reminded that there will be "wonders in the heaven above and signs on the earth below" (Acts 2:19), and that one result of the outpouring of God's Spirit will be that God's servants, both men and women, will prophesy.

God intended that his children should be a prophetic people. There will be those who come to the fore, recognised by the Church as having a prophetic ministry. (I believe this should ideally be affirmed by the local church, then by the wider Church in some sense, if the ministry becomes national or international.) There are different gifts but we are encouraged by St Paul eagerly to desire the greater gifts, including prophecy (1 Corinthians 12:28,31,39). Obviously the checks and balances referred to in 1 Corinthians 12–14 and elsewhere in Scripture must be observed so that all is done decently and in order, and guidelines are followed for "weighing" prophecy.

Jesus himself, as the Word of God, was the greatest prophet of all time. In the prophetic role of "forthteller", speaking God's "now" word into a situation, his words pierced the very heart of man. But he was also a "foreteller" and his predictions of what was and is to come are the clearest we have of future events, using little of the more apocalyptic language which characterises such writers as St John in the book of Revelation.

It was the obvious intention of Jesus to give his disciples, and all who would later become disciples, clear warnings of what was to come. All three synoptic gospels record Jesus' teaching about the future at some length (Matthew 24 and 25, Mark 13, Luke 21), showing that he took some considerable time revealing these things to his disciples just before the events of his Passion. When one combines this with other references in John's gospel, in a number of epistles, the book of Revelation, and of course, large sections of the Old Testament, it seems rather strange, to say the least, that future prophecy has been a subject neglected by Christians for so long, apart from those who would be regarded as "extremists".

We do not avoid doctrines such as the Trinity or the Atonement just because they are complex or because some people twist them into heresy. Perhaps the enemy is successfully deceiving millions of Christians into ignoring the important subject of eschatology so that they will be unprepared or deceived. Evangelical, charismatic and traditionalist Christian leaders need to affirm loud and clear at least the basic doctrines of the Last Things, lest the Christian public be lulled into a false sense of security, leading to apathy.

New Age eschatology

The New Agers have their eschatology. The devil will in this last decade of the millennium ensure that "end of the world fever" is spread like an epidemic so that millions will follow this false prophet and that false christ through fascination or fear. Christians dare not just warn people of the dangers. We must also proclaim the biblical truth about the Last Things in a definite way. The time has gone for hedging our bets, beating about the bush, or whatever other suitable metaphor comes to mind. Even

142

the ordinary secular world, let alone the world of the occult, is usually more prophetic than the Church about major events such as disasters, the significance of what is happening in the Communist bloc, etc. A variety of newspapers, including *The Times* and the *Daily Mail*, have carried numerous such articles recently.

Necessity for Christian teaching

Christian leaders need to reaffirm biblical teaching on Christ's victory over death, to preach more on the reality and joy of heaven and to warn of judgement. They need to prepare God's people for the Second Coming of Jesus, the destruction of the old order, the new heaven and earth, and to explain the signs leading up to these events. We could be near to the most cataclysmic events of all time, yet from the majority of pulpits and platforms there is a resounding silence.

The Christian public is longing for more direction on these matters. Optional seminars at the major UK Christian event, Spring Harvest in 1990, which had been tucked into odd corners of the programme, on such subjects as "The New Age" and "The End of the World", were packed out. Lists of subscribers for magazines on prophetic matters grow weekly.

Jesus commanded us to "keep watch, because you do not know the day or the hour" (Matthew 25:13). I have no difficulty at all in taking literally the description of the Second Coming as found in 1 Thessalonians 4 and elsewhere. I would anyway, because of my view of Scripture and my assessment that it does not fit into the category of poetry, but of straightforward prediction. But also, at the age of twelve, I experienced the only true

143

vision I have had, as if the Second Coming were actually taking place there and then, and I was being caught up from my room through the window, which though closed, proved irrelevant, to meet my Lord in the air, which was filled with indescribable light and music. From that point on I have always dismissed theories that the only way everyone could see him would be if they all happened to be watching a television screen! I just know with certainty that everyone at that time will see him in an instant. The major significance of this experience, however, was to give me a sense of urgency about serving God, which has never left me.

The teaching of Scripture is that the Second Coming could happen at any time (in one sense) to an "ordinary" generation of people carrying on their normal lives. In other words, it could happen in our lifetime to you and to me. Even though the Bible makes that absolutely clear in numerous references, and denounces those who are not ready, most Christians have a mental blockage over the matter. This is partly psychological – we just find it so hard to imagine such a stupendous, supernatural event involving us whilst we are alive. This is a normal reaction, for it is difficult enough when we contemplate a major change in our lives, such as having a first child, or moving to another country, to imagine it actually happening in reality. The other reason is that although Jesus warns us that the Second Coming will take place at a time we least expect, when people are doing normal things (Matthew 24:36–41), we find that hard to relate to the horrific events depicted in the book of Revelation. How could people possibly be living normal lives when such terrible things are happening on earth that men are in agony and curse God? (e.g. Revelation 16:8–14, with verse 15 placing these appalling disasters firmly in the context of the Second Coming: "Behold, I come like a thief! Blessed is he who stays awake . . ."). Part of the answer here is the amazing ability of man to carry on some semblance of normal life in the most adverse circumstances, such as the blitz on London in World War II, or in Beirut today.

Another important part of the answer is to be found when we have a better understanding of predictive prophecy in the Bible. The approach which has done so much damage is to draw up a detailed "timetable" of future events based on a particular interpretation of the prophecies as yet unfulfilled. It is possible to become totally convinced by one view based on Scripture, until someone else comes along with another equally plausible view also based on the Bible. It is this conviction that the biblical prophecies are intended to show us a specific order of events which has led to some being obsessed with their viewpoint, others being confused even to the extent of closing their minds to the importance of biblical predictions.

Three reasons for biblical predictive prophecy

It seems to me that we need to look in a new way at what the Holy Spirit was seeking to achieve by including so much predictive prophecy in the Bible. He firstly wanted the people of God to be aware, at the time when God intervenes in this world in a particular way, *that indeed it is God*, by notifying us beforehand, e.g. the prediction of the fall of Jerusalem, Luke 21:24, (fulfilled in AD 70). Secondly, as God's intervention always either invites a response from man (e.g. the Cross and Resurrection) or marks the end of the possibility of such a response (e.g.

the Last Judgement) the Holy Spirit needed to warn us beforehand *to urge us to make the right response*. Thirdly, in some cases if the prediction is about judgement and men respond by repentance, then the *judgement may be averted*. The book of Jonah demonstrates a positive example of this in relation to Nineveh. However, sometimes things have gone too far for judgement to be reversed even by repentance, as in the case of Israel before the first exile (Jeremiah 14:11,12), and of course this will be the case in the matter of the final show-down between good and evil, God and the devil.

These reasons for biblical predictive prophecy should in themselves provide sufficient motive for ensuring that the people of God are well taught about such things. It is essential that we know, as events unfold, that it is God who is intervening; it is vital that we are prepared to respond in wonder or repentance or whatever is appropriate; it is crucial that we understand that in some cases judgement may be averted or postponed if we turn back to God and intercede for his mercy.

Two keys to understanding biblical prophecy

The role of the person with the ministry of teaching is to explain where prophecies have been fulfilled and where they have yet to be fulfilled. He should have an understanding, amongst other things, of two special features of biblical prophecies. I have called these the "concertina effect" and the "multiple reference aspect". *The concertina effect* is where a biblical prophet would alert us of events to come but would see them dimly, all bunched up together, not necessarily recognising that it could be a long-drawn-out process. It was as if he were looking from a vantage point at a succession of mountain tops, either not noticing or not mentioning the long valleys of time in between. An example of this would be Jesus' prophecies in Luke 21:24–27. Within a few sentences he refers to an event to happen within a generation (the fall of Jerusalem AD 70). He then predicts that there will be an end to the tragedy of Jerusalem being trampled on by the Gentiles. (Some would see this as fulfilled at least partially in 1967, 1900 years after the first part of the prophecy.) He goes on to speak of signs in the heaven and on the earth, men fainting from terror, and the Son of Man coming in power and glory (obviously still future).

The reason for this apparent vagueness about the time factor was of course that God wants his people constantly to be alert, watching, listening, discerning and trusting.

The multiple reference aspect of prophecy may be illustrated by the prediction in Joel 2:28–32. Peter claimed that this was fulfilled at Pentecost (Acts 2:16–21). This first outpouring of the Spirit was a dramatic initial fulfilment. There have been other occasions throughout history when some would see other fulfilments (even though in some cases people involved later lapsed into extremism or became heretical). There was the Montanist movement in the second century onwards, the first Quakers in the seventeenth century, the traditional Pentecostals at the beginning of this century, and of course the later Charismatic Movement. Yet there will also be future fulfilment, particularly in connection with the verses about signs in the heavens and on the earth. One of the implications of multiple reference in prophecies is that it is untenable for whole generations of Christians to dismiss large sections of biblical prophecy as far too remote to concern them.

The ministry of prophecy today

The role of the person with a ministry of prophecy today is rather different from that of the teacher of biblical prophecy. Any Christian may of course ask for the gift of the word of prophecy from time to time, which will mainly be for edification of the Church (1 Corinthians 14:3,4). There will be those who will develop this gift until it is recognised by the Church as a prophetic ministry. It should be obvious that no new truth will be added to Scripture. God's plan of salvation and all the truths about his nature and other major doctrines have been revealed in his Word. This includes eschatology. St Peter tells us very clearly that prophecy of Scripture was completely pure in origin. "Above all you must understand that no prophecy of Scripture came about by the prophet's own interpretation. For prophecy never had its origin in the will of man, but men spoke from God as they were carried along by the Holy Spirit" (2 Peter 1:20,21).

Post-New Testament prophecy can never be in the same category but always subject to Scripture. Nevertheless, we must not play down the ministry of the prophet, which St Paul makes clear in Ephesians 4:11-13 is still essential for the Church. The writers and early readers of the New Testament would have understood the two major aspects of the ministry of a prophet: forthtelling and foretelling. Nowhere are we told that the predictive aspect will cease (until all prophecy ceases altogether, "when perfection comes", 1 Corinthians 13:9,10).

The emphasis in 1 Corinthians 14 is on the strengthening, encouraging and comforting side of prophecy and, with Ephesians 4, underlines that this ministry is for the body of Christ to be built up. This has mistakenly been taken so often as meaning that present-day prophecy is to consist of words of encouragement. This error has led to a dilution of this vital ministry to the extent that words of "prophecy" are more often than not insipid and virtually pointless. Yet in 1 Corinthians 14:24,25 St Paul tells us that prophecies may convict a sinner and lay bare the secrets of his heart. One could take this beyond the individual and point out that a church would not be "built up" if there are things which first need to be removed, or changed, lest the building be shaky. The true ministry of prophecy into the local church should therefore be very perceptive and courageous, warning, exposing, tearing down if necessary, before building up. In fact, in the Old Testament those who only ever prophesied peace were usually false prophets.

One could take this a step further and recognise that it is impossible to build up if only the present is seen. No one builds a house or an office block without considering the future needs for which it is intended. Similarly, the Holy Spirit, who is outside of time, in order to build up the Church through those with a prophetic ministry, will communicate future needs and direction to prophets. Agabus predicted the famine in the reign of Claudius so that the Church could take appropriate action, and he also foretold Paul's captivity (Acts 11:28, 21:10), although the Church mistook the application of this. In both references other prophets or prophetesses are mentioned in the previous verse, showing that Agabus was not unique.

Predictions by modern prophets could be for an individual, or a local church, or the wider Church in an area, country or even the world. Old Testament prophets spoke in the main to the people of God, but also had prophecies for pagan nations. All this range may be seen by a brief look at some of Jeremiah's prophecies where, having prophesied about Jerusalem earlier in his ministry, and to an individual (Baruch, in chapter 45), he goes on to speak against Egypt, Philistia, Moab, Ammon, Edom, Damascus, Arabia, Elam and Babylon (chapters 46–51). It is possible and certainly not ruled out by Scripture that Christian prophets could be used in this way. All of these prophecies would either be bringing Scripture into a situation as God's "now" word, or could be "extra" biblical as long as they are not inconsistent with Scripture.

We should certainly expect that men and women, recognised as having a prophetic ministry, will have insight in connection with the predictive prophecies of the Bible which are as yet unfulfilled. Just as Peter stood up on the day of Pentecost and said with authority: "*This is that* which was spoken by the prophet Joel" (Acts 2:16 AV), *so we would expect God to anoint men and women with similar authority to interpret the signs of the times in relation to Scriptural prophecies.*

The true prophetic ministry will therefore be very powerful and, if heeded, be an important instrument in God's purposes for the life of an individual, the local church, the wider Church and possibly even nations.

It is one of the major weaknesses of the Charismatic Movement that prophecy has not been given its rightful place but has usually been reduced to the level of helpful thoughts. People are so afraid of false prophecy that they have not been prepared to take risks of faith. It is vital to distinguish between false prophecy and fleshly prophecy. The false prophet would be one either directly inspired by a demon, or with selfish or warped motives – to glorify himself, manipulate others, curry favour or even line his pockets. This is very different from someone who is embarking on a prophetic ministry or is even "fully fledged" but occasionally makes a mistake, or begins in the Spirit and gets a bit carried away, ending in the flesh. This could happen to any true prophet from time to time, as no one is perfect, and one should not expect the same purity of hearing God as for the writers of Scripture. It does not invalidate his whole ministry. Incidentally, the actual "words of prophecy" in fairly short "messages" will only be the tip of an iceberg for a person with a true prophetic ministry. He or she will be giving direction amongst the eldership of a church (to be weighed by them), or preaching prophetic sermons, writing prophetic articles or books about wider issues.

I sense that God's intention is for the whole area of true prophetic ministry to be restored to its rightful place in the Church today, as history moves to its climax. But I also have a sense of grief that the enemy is going to try to hijack it.

The difference between prophecy and ESP

It is vital that we know the biblical tests for the true prophet and hold them together. Prophecy is totally different from ESP (extra sensory perception). Anyone with this ability needs to renounce it and be prepared for God to give a different gift from that of prophecy if he sees fit. ESP is that uncanny sense that something is about to happen, usually (although not necessarily) something gloomy or tragic, and yet the knowledge is virtually pointless. It only brings fear or pride – the person who receives it or the people it concerns have no power to avert the tragedy, nothing constructive comes of it and God is not glorified.

The true prophet will always have as his motive the glory of God. Any predictions will have some point, usually giving time for a response from those who listen. This inevitably means that if judgement is predicted but God gives time for repentance and that takes place, the judgement may be averted and therefore the prophecy will not actually come true in the original terms of the prediction. This is the dilemma of the prophet. It is vital he is seen to be a true prophet, one of the Scriptural conditions being that his prophecies come true (Deuteronomy 18:22), yet if the response is appropriate there is the risk that there is no way of proving what might have been. The greatest temptation for the true prophet, when he foresees judgement, is to want that judgement to take place in order to prove him right. That is why Jonah sulked when God had compassion on Nineveh after the people repented. After all, he hadn't wanted to give the prophecy in the first place. He had run away and only got round to saying "yes" to God after the great whale episode. He had then risked the wrath of the mighty king of Assyria, wandering through his capital proclaiming disaster. Surely his "reward" would be that he would see his prophecy come true. But amazingly the king and population fasted and repented, and to Jonah's dismay, God averted disaster and so none of his predictions came true. Poor Jonah. After all that! God's answer to the angry prophet was to encourage him to share his heart of love for the 120,000 people of Nineveh.

The true Christian prophet has nothing if he does not have love. He is a resounding gong or a clanging cymbal (1 Corinthians 13). All true prophets will have responded to the divine call to this ministry with reluctance. One would have to be twisted in mind to want to go around proclaiming words from God which could include extremely traumatic insights. Having got over the hurdle of responding with reluctance, the next temptation is to pride when one gets a prophecy with a bit more bite to it than "Bless you my children". It is essential that the temptation to gloat over discerning gloom and doom to come is resisted, and that the prophet proceeds no further without experiencing something of the grief of the heart of God. The next stage, as mentioned above, is to embrace the glorious possibility that repentance by those who listen will avert the prophesied judgement (in other words, to risk there being no proof of the prediction being accurate). This is an exception to the criterion of the true prophet in Deuteronomy 18:22, "If what a prophet proclaims in the name of the Lord does not take place or come true, that is a message the Lord has not spoken." An example would be the insight that the New Age is, or at least will merge into, the End Time deceit. The temptation which can become severe is to seize on everything which appears to confirm that view and almost to be reluctant to intercede against the New Age, or to fail to rejoice when there are victories in overcoming it. Obviously, if there were to be massive Christian awareness and spiritual warfare against it, then the enemy would have to retreat and regroup. He might make a come-back using different terminology, yet the heart of the New Age, "the lie" that we are gods, remains the enemy's ultimate weapon. The fact also remains that there has to be a final showdown between the kingdoms of darkness and light at a point in time decreed by God, to bring to an end the pride of the world, the flesh and the devil. *The other exception is to be found in Deuteronomy 13:1-5, where a ''prophet's'' predictions, including those about signs and wonders, come true, but he is in fact leading people astray from God and his word, and so is a false prophet. I believe we shall see a lot of this in the days to come, including within the renewal movement.*

There are other tests of a prophet, such as his character and whether he has a listening attitude to God, but the main caution is to beware the self-styled prophet who comes from nowhere and inflicts himself on others, without church backing, and who is not willing for his prophecies to be weighed.

What then should we expect to hear in these days through modern prophets, so that the children of God, who have ears to hear (i.e. who want to be a prophetic people) are up to date in their understanding of God's purposes? I refer particularly to predictive prophecies relating biblical eschatology to current events. If the detailed timetable of future events is "out", what should be in its place?

The signs of the first and second coming of Jesus

Surely if we are expecting the Second Advent of Jesus, what happened before and at his First Advent in terms of prophecy and discernment should provide major guidelines. Those who formed to their own satisfaction a clear and detailed timetable and view of the coming Messiah were to be disappointed. God kept them waiting for four centuries with no further prophetic word. When the Messiah came he was either not recognised, or rejected eventually by those who had interpreted the prophecies as referring to one who would conquer the conquerors of the people of God. Those who recongised the infant Jesus as the Messiah (apart from the shepherds and the magi who were assisted by a heavenly choir or a star) were two old prophets, Simeon and Anna. They knew their Scriptures, prayed, waited and recognised the prompting of the Holy Spirit at the right moment. It was thirty years later before Peter confessed Jesus to be the Christ, but then only to deny him. God chose those to whom he would reveal the risen Jesus, but the religious leaders and rulers of the people were mostly not among them, because they had misinterpreted prophecy and in fact crucified the Messiah. The sins of the whole world, Jew and Gentile alike, took Jesus to the cross, so there is absolutely no cause for the terrible sin of anti-semitism. I need to say that because of what I am going on to say. The fact is, the almighty God viewed so seriously the failure of the religious leadership to discern that his prophetic words about the Messiah in the Old Testament were fulfilled in Jesus, that his chosen people were sent into exile for nearly two thousand years.(Of course, they went beyond failure in discernment, to outright rejection of God's Son, to the extent of defiance in calling for his blood to be on them and their children (Matthew 27:25).) Yet all they had to go on was the word of God in prophecy, and discernment at the time from the Holy Spirit for those who had ears to hear, to link the man Jesus with the prophecies.

Similarly, that is all we have today to interpret the signs preceding the Second Coming of Jesus. Every eye will see that event – but will we miss the fact that we are living in the days leading up to the Second Coming? We "only" have the prophecies in the Bible and the discernment given to God's people by the Holy Spirit, particularly to those with a prophetic ministry.

Prophets are arising who have a wider than local ministry but not one has the whole picture. It is important to remember that if a predictive prophecy is from God it is not just foretelling, but as it is spoken out is used by God to accomplish the very thing predicted, just as when Ezekiel prophesied to the dry bones. The prophetic ministry therefore carries a heavy responsibility. Some might prophesy into their denominations, as Tony does. Some might prophesy into the ecumenical scene. Some might have insight into interfaith activities. An increasing number are discerning the significance of the New Age. Some might speak into aspects of the life of their nation (e.g. pro-life issues), or to the church in a country about God's attitude to that nation. We have yet to reach the stage where a nation takes notice of its Christian prophets in any meaningful sense. Some might prophesy about Israel, or the USSR or the international scene.

Those with a prophetic ministry should be careful to go a step at a time, not to prophesy beyond the measure of faith they have been given. But I believe that all prophets should speak out against the *background* of an awareness of the bigger things God is doing in the world today leading up to the Second Coming. Yet there should be humility to balance the sense of urgency, with the acknowledgement that we only dimly perceive the wider scene, and do not have it all sewn up.

An over-view of End Time events

I would expect true prophets today to proclaim that God is preparing his Bride, but that will mean both the joy and pain of the purifying fire of revival. They will see that Joel 2:32 must have its final fulfilment – that "everyone who calls on the name of the Lord will be saved". Yet they will hold that in tension with the terrible things the enemy is being permitted to do, including great deception even of the elect, "if that were possible" (Matthew 24:24). Even worse, "Because of the increase of wickedness, the love of most will grow cold" (Matthew 24:12). Who can square Joel 2:32 and Matthew 24:12? Will revival precede apostasy? Or will the two take place together, as I tend to think? We only "see through a glass darkly" as yet.

Since writing the above I have been to a mainstream charismatic conference where the speakers were drawn from the Anglican church and the House churches, amongst others. They included well-known leaders in renewal. I was very disturbed to find that, to a man, they were all speaking about the wonderful revival to come, without a word about judgement, except to dismiss the possibility. I am convinced that such a triumphalist approach is completely out of harmony with biblical prophecy. It is not only unscriptural, but unloving to the people of God to fail to warn them of what is to come.

Many of the "signs" have always happened – wars, famines, earthquakes, plagues and persecutions – but there will apparently be an increase in frequency and severity. In fact the newsreader on Radio 4 in June 1990, speaking after the terrible Iranian earthquake with its massive loss of life, said "Earthquakes with their dreadful toll are becoming more commonplace." Israel will be prominent on the scene and at some stage after the Gospel of the kingdom has been preached to the whole world, the full number of the Gentiles will come in and then all Israel will be saved (Romans 11), i.e. a remnant, surviving after terrible war, who will look on the one they pierced (Zechariah 12:10). This will have significance for the nations of the world. A further feature towards the very end will be the great tribulation, with the emergence of the ultimate manifestation of the antichrist. The heavenly bodies will be shaken and Jesus will come again. I am not attempting to give a chronology but just picking out often repeated themes from the words of Jesus, some of the epistles, Revelation, Ezekiel, Daniel, etc. Some see the Rapture mentioned in 1 Thessalonians immediately followed by the Return to the Mount of Olives (Zechariah 14), with perhaps chosen believers ruling with Christ for a time on this earth. I personally think the millennium will be totally different from anything we imagine, confounding all our expectations. It could perhaps be a very brief demonstration of the total sovereignty of Jesus over nations and creation, for a thousand years can be as but a day with God. Then could come the events of the destruction of the old order, the Last Judgement and the new heavens and earth.

We are not meant at this stage to sort out the exact order and how it all fits together, and I believe we should actually resist the temptation to bring our natural desire for logical order to bear on the whole scene. Nevertheless, there are many clear signs that we are near to all these events unfolding. The Second Coming will be a surprise but it should not be a shock.

There is very little amongst the signs of the End that is unfulfilled, or that would be impossible to be fulfilled within a generation. World events are unfolding so rapidly and dramatically that even the most astute political commentator is left stunned. That is not to deny that it could all take much longer. The Lord's timing is not ours, and his thoughts are higher than ours.

We must be definite about what is clear, we must also draw attention with humility to what may happen, yet is complex and not fully understood. We must warn, watch and pray. We should be prophetic either in our understanding, or if such is our ministry, in speaking boldly into the situation about which God has given us a prophetic message. We should hear with increasing frequency and authority from our leading prophetic preachers the words: "*This* (which you now see) is *that*" (which was predicted in Scripture).

Meanwhile we do not continually gaze up into heaven until Jesus returns, but rather get on with the urgent task of extending God's Kingdom through the Church, before it is too late.

CHAPTER EIGHT

God and the Church

As a leader in the parish of Hawkwell in south-east Essex for over fifteen years, I have noticed that some of the illustrations used in the New Testament to describe the church have become reality to us, at different stages in our corporate development.

The church as a "building"

At first the emphasis was on the church as a spiritual *building*. We became aware that in many cases a local church is built sloppily, even thrown together in haphazard fashion. It might appear to be lively, even bursting at the seams. But the Architect's plans have been forgotten, there is little vision as to what the end result should look like or what its function is. In other cases there is a rigid, manmade structure. The Master Architect has not been consulted; at best he is asked to bless the plans of man, normally drawn up in endless committee meetings. There may be plenty of activity, but each group is usually run as it was in the beginning, is now and ever shall be. The breath of the Spirit hardly ever blows through such an organisation. Change is viewed with deep-seated suspicion and if made is carried out either in an underhand way by an oligarchy, or after much heated discussion and dissension, by democratic vote. Theocracy, or rule by God, is never even considered, or else regarded as unattainable, particularly within the historic denominations.

Yet Jesus said, ''I will build my church'' (Matthew 16:18). We realised in our early years in Hawkwell that if he was not allowed to build, then at best we would only construct something which looked good to the eye of man, but in fact would not endure for eternity.

Slowly, painfully, the Holy Spirit taught us principles of building. Little did we realise in those first traumatic years that God was allowing the process for us to be particularly protracted and painful, because there was a wider than local, even a wider than national, ministry at stake. We were later to teach similar principles to churches in (at present) eight nations.

We had always understood that Jesus was to be the foundation of this building. ''For no one can lay any foundation other than the one already laid, which is Jesus Christ'' (1 Corinthians 3:11). Yet we soon realised that although the Gospel had been faithfully preached by a number of rectors before my husband arrived, and he majored on it in his ministry, only perhaps fifty per cent of the congregation appeared to have a living faith, whereas a considerable number who came week by week made virtually no progress spiritually. It seemed that evangelistic sermons made little impact. The only answer was the personal approach. Some are naturally gifted in this, but that was not so in our case. We therefore found the training of ''Evangelism Explosion'' so useful, for it taught us how to get beyond general conversation or talking about pastoral needs, right to the heart of the matter. We learned to ask leading questions in a sensitive way

162

which enabled us to discover whether an individual was trusting in Jesus Christ, or in good works. In the privacy of the home we were able to lead someone who had perhaps been coming to church for years, into at least assurance of salvation, or even to enter into a personal relationship with Jesus for the first time.

Gradually we were able to reach out to those on the fringe of the congregation, which actually proved to be the most fruitful aspect of our evangelistic endeavours. People who came once a month to a family service, parents who "sent their children to Sunday school", or those who had suffered bereavement, responded readily when we shared the Gospel with them, whereas some of our "regulars" proved to be stony ground. At that stage we got a bit stuck in evangelism, as the "fringe" either became deeply involved in the life of the church, or turned away. We went through an unfruitful period until we realised the need for "pre-evangelism" and "presence evangelism", as well as the direct challenge. We had to learn to become involved in the community. This was not just in order to win people for Jesus, but because it is important to care for folk at their point of physical, emotional or practical need, whether or not they respond spiritually. We now have a constantly changing "fringe", as people on the outer edges of church life are drawn into the centre and others from outside the congregation take their place.

> For I am building a people of power,
> And I am making a people of praise;
> Who will move through this land by my Spirit,
> And glorify my precious name.

Not perhaps the most profound of choruses, but one which came to mean a lot to us as a church in the late

1970s. By then some of us were entering into the gifts of the Spirit, and we dimly perceived that this simple song was becoming prophetic for us. There were other prophecies about the importance of building carefully on the foundation, ensuring there were no weaknesses in those first layers of bricks, or else the superstructure would crack.

At this point it is important to stress that we have never been taken up with the actual physical buildings in which we worship. Many a time we could have been sidetracked to take this diversion, which is so tempting to many clergy and pastors. After all, we have one thirteenth-century parish church building and a larger, more modern but poorly constructed daughter church. Yet apart from the miraculous provision of a church house, the usual upkeep of the two churches, a projected modest extension to our tiny ancient church, and the necessity of replacing a grotty church hall, it has never seemed right to pay much attention to the buildings. Perhaps when people visit Hawkwell from all over the world they are surprised to see our rather inadequate "plant". One of our congregations meets in a rented school hall. Hopefully our visitors get the message that the extension of God's Kingdom has never depended on, and can even be impeded by, attention to buildings. We all know of some magnificent church buildings, the dream perhaps of some clergyman or pastor with a successful ministry even in the recent past, which today are almost empty, echoing vaults. We know too that, from all accounts, the Church in China has grown to somewhere between fifty and one hundred million believers, with scarcely a church building to their name. Yet still we do not learn.

By God's grace we concentrated on the true church – the development of the believing community. The Holy Spirit taught us that we would achieve little without corporate prayer, but that true prayer begins by discovering what is on God's heart before entering into intercession. There has to be listening as well as talking. If we were to allow Jesus to build his Church in Hawkwell; if we were to co-operate with the Master Architect in our different roles: surveyors, foremen, bricklayers, etc., then we needed to follow his instructions. We discovered that all the basic principles were there already in God's word. But it was also important to hear in prayer through God's "now" word to us, about such matters as priorities, order of events, any demolition, or strengthening of weak areas, and inclusion of special details for us in Hawkwell.

So we learned how to prepare ourselves in prayer: through worship, repentance, resisting the enemy and asking for the empowering of the Holy Spirit. For us the most important preparation was learning to submit our own ideas about what to pray for, how to pray for it and even how we expected God to answer. The voice of the flesh, of self, can be so dominant that it can drown the still, small whisper of the voice of God.

We made many mistakes in our first "listening" style prayer group, sometimes failing to hear God at all, sometimes hearing his directives but then losing our sense of direction halfway through the meeting. On other occasions we just knew that we had tuned right into the centre of God's purposes, whether for an individual, the church or the nation. At that time we had an eldership of five men, and there were half a dozen women in our one experimental prayer group. If we believed the Holy Spirit was sharing with the prayer group something of a prophetic nature about the development of the life of Hawkwell church, the ladies took care to convey this as soon as possible to the eldership. Thankfully, men are now just as involved as women in the prayer life of the church, and the prayer cells have multiplied. On the other side, women are more affirmed in leading roles, although in Hawkwell we still believe that if a man is in the role of presiding elder, that is more in harmony with God's order, particularly for the purpose of spiritual protection.

As I have quoted in another context, when God called Jeremiah he said to him, "See, today I appoint you over nations and kingdoms, to uproot and tear down, to destroy and overthrow, to build and to plant" (Jeremiah 1:10). In the first seven years in Hawkwell it seemed to us, in a similar way, that we were spending most of our time tackling negative issues rather than dealing with positive construction. We now understand that local churches of any denomination or none, in some cases for decades, in others for centuries, have so often operated at a subnormal level compared with the teaching of the New Testament. When challenged to live by the biblical norm, this can seem abnormal, even radical. There is therefore resistance to challenge and change.

Our church appeared in the early years to be capable of harmful division over almost anything you could mention, from big things like renewal, to mundane things like church furniture. We then discovered that there was the same root cause to all the division. It was a matter of the heart. For the real division was between those who were hungry and thirsty for God's rule in their own life and the life of the church, and those who were not. There is an old saying that you can lead a horse to water but you cannot make it drink. We tried to lead many "horses" in those days – some bolted almost immediately, some got as far as the water. I have to confess that in our enthusiasm to see people led to the Lord or baptised in the Spirit, or envisioned about the true nature of the Church and the extension of God's Kingdom, we perhaps even tried to drag some a little further than they wanted to go. But in any case some refused to drink. Others rushed off to their own little pond, in isolation from the mainstream of God's purposes. Sadly, we had to let them go, with many tears. Praise God for the many who either slowly and cautiously, or eagerly and thirstily, drank what the Holy Spirit was offering – something more like the biblical standard of Christian and church life.

Slowly we learned that courageous leadership is necessary. That does not mean absence of fear, but pressing on in awe of God rather than fear of man. One thing is certain, if those involved in the building of the Church are not prepared for the cost of getting rid of what is manmade or badly built now, it will be disposed of hereafter, when we stand before the judgement seat of Christ (1 Corinthians 3:10–15). That can mean making some unpopular decisions. Any Christian leader who is not prepared to lay down his reputation now, and all ambition for success measured by human standards, will find himself very ashamed on that day.

In Hawkwell we made a deliberate act of handing over to God the grain of wheat represented by "our church". We told God we were prepared for the husk to die so that new life could spring from the inner core of what remained. The old prayerless ways had to go, man-pleasing "worship", human methods, even some organisations and groups which the Spirit had finished with. Disunity, cliques, low standards of discipleship, the one-man ministry – all these things had to change, and much more besides. We constantly prayed the simple prayer: "Lord, transform or remove." By that we were pleading with God to change heart attitudes, but sadly in some cases it was not attitudes which were removed but people. Either God removed them in a variety of ways, including change of job, or some chose to go. It is easy to pray for God to act in a sovereign way, but not so easy when God tells a leader to take action in dealing with unbiblical behaviour. The overall leadership, in perhaps a dozen times in the fifteen years we have been in the parish, had to follow right through the course of action recommended by Jesus in Matthew 18:15–17. This meant approaching a church member privately, and if this proved unfruitful the leader would take one or two objective church members with him to assess the situation. Most matters are resolved at stage one, and this happens regularly in a gentle, confidential way between member and member, leader and leader, or leader and member. It is all good and healthy, the biblical way to resolve disputes and hurts. But if we are to be truly biblical, leaders must in a small number of cases be prepared sensitively to follow the other steps outlined by Jesus himself in those verses.

In these ways the Holy Spirit showed us what it means to allow Jesus to build his Church. The foundation had to be right, we needed to know the Architect's plans in the Bible and to listen in prayer for detailed instructions. We had to be prepared to deal with any weaknesses and especially in the early days clear away rubbish. The whole process was not a project which could be completed and then left. As with any building there is a need for upkeep, changes and extension. We therefore try to continue to listen to God, as our prayer cells have multiplied. Each prayer cell prays for an aspect of the life of the church (worship, young people, healing, etc.) and on alternate weeks for wider mission. We have always emphasised that these groups should be outward-looking, as the great temptation is to end up praying for one another's needs every week. We try to keep open lines of communication by encouraging prayer reports to be made by group leaders, and acted on, where appropriate, by the overall leadership. We often also call the church together, or just the leaders, for evenings of prayer about specific matters for which we need guidance. These are usually highlights in the life of our church. People prepare carefully beforehand and come prepared to share some relevant Scriptures or discernment. We reach an amazing level of harmony at such times, so that it seems good to the Holy Spirit and to us to take a particular course of action.

The church as a "Body"

Gradually the concept of the local church as a *Body* came to have even more significance than the metaphor of building. In Hawkwell we "inherited" a number of gifted people but there was almost total absence of unity. Arms and legs, toes and fingers, ears and eyes, were off doing their own thing – not a pretty sight. God showed us how to achieve unity before we dared risk diversity. It is so unfortunate that when many churches try to enter into every-member ministry, the gifts of the Spirit, or even such a simple concept as setting up housegroups, these can become factors not of growth but of disintegration. The reason is that clergy or pastors are dealing with a divided situation in the first place. This may be partially concealed, but is soon revealed as more freedom is allowed. Sometimes this can lead to a desperately serious situation which has been the downfall of many a Christian minister.

Before we went to Hawkwell, the previous rector and his wife warned Tony and me that the church members were at loggerheads. We struggled for seven years against the divisive attitudes, taking the steps I have outlined above and also engaging in spiritual warfare, which we shall examine later. Eventually we realised that short of a supernatural act of God such as revival (though even revival creates rivals and dissenters), or something less welcome such as serious persecution (which tends to drive together true believers and removes nominalism), we needed to set about teaching unity in a deliberate and practical way.

This more positive approach to unity coincided with the second seven-year phase of our ministry in Hawkwell, beginning in 1982. We recognised the need to summarise what the New Testament teaches about the Body of Christ and to invite all the church members to study a course expounding those principles. Compared with other major doctrines, we had been so hazy about the church. Sunday by Sunday we declared in the Creed our basic beliefs on major doctrine in summary form. These doctrines were expounded from the pulpit and in other contexts. We understood those truths imperfectly, but would soon detect any major heresy. Yet even though on this basis a superstructure of living stones was being erected, we were failing one another by being less than definite as to the aims of our corporate life. So my husband wrote down *The Vision of the Nature and Mission of the Local Church*. This was a summary of New Testament teaching about the Church and the responsibility of the individual within it. We called it a Vision as the word seemed to convey an ideal to aim towards.

Many people have visions – some in the literal sense of that word, a kind of "waking dream", a personal revelation conveying a message. Others have a vision in a more general sense – a dream or a goal of life. For us this was a corporate vision in the latter sense, but in order to avoid the opinions of man, this "Vision" summarises biblical teaching and is thoroughly substantiated by Scripture in the course expounding it. We have a longer version, but in summary form the Vision is of a united fellowship, one in heart and mind, all of whose members are:

1. Wholeheartedly committed to Jesus Christ as Saviour and Lord.
2. Baptised and regular at Communion.
3. Experiencing the power of the Holy Spirit.
4. Doers of the Word, not hearers only.
5. Living adventurously by faith in God's protection and provision.
6. Seeking holiness before God.
7. Involved in disciplined intercession and "hearing" God.
8. Offering wholehearted praise and worship to God.

9. Committed to each other in unity and love; loyal to and trusting each other including the leaders; encouraging each other; open to loving correction on biblical issues, sharing needs and possessions.
10. Discerning one another's gifts and practising "every-member ministry".
11. Engaged in spiritual warfare.
12. Involved in evangelism, by love, word and power, in the light of the return of Christ.

We now knew what we were aiming at together, which is a major step towards unity. However, we faced a problem. It wasn't so much that some folk felt this was too high an ideal. That showed true humility and usually careful explanation helped. We explained that it was Scriptural teaching, therefore we can by God's grace at least aim towards it, helping one another. There were also one or two who disputed certain points, particularly in No.9, and in each case it was a matter of expounding Scripture so that the choice was whether to follow the word of God or not. No, our main problem was not with those who were fearful or the minority who disputed certain points. It was the more subtle danger that the vast majority *said* they agreed with every word, yet we knew that in a small number of cases they did not mean it. After all, we had been a divided church. Even in 1982, seven years on in our time in Hawkwell, there were some who had no intention of even trying to follow Christ wholeheartedly. Or perhaps they shunned involvement in intercession, or were unwilling for greater freedom in worship. There was disloyalty by a minority towards leaders. Some had no desire to discover and use God given gifts, or else they inflicted their natural gifts on the church, gifts which they were not prepared for God to refine.

It became clear that we had to make a deliberate effort to move beyond this state of affairs which is typical of so many churches, and yet subnormal by New Testament standards. We therefore invited all those who had studied the Vision in our Commitment Course now known as "called to serve", to make a corporate public act of commitment to working towards the implementation of the Vision, by the grace of God. The church council approved this step, and of the well over eighty per cent of the congregation who chose to study the Course, the vast majority made an act of dedication in a special service. These folk then became members of weekly area home ministry groups.

Within a year from that turning point, most of our major problems over disunity were at an end. Christians moving into the parish, or new Christians, all went through similar steps, and the whole idea became accepted as the basic norm for our corporate life. We believe that the Holy Spirit revealed these simple steps to enable us to become more like the Body of Christ. It was soon evident that in no sense had this been some sort of system which was more to do with procedure rather than reality. To safeguard against that we always stressed the grace and power of God, and the importance of prayer. It gradually dawned on us that we were seeing a miracle take place before our eyes.

In place of that disunited congregation, we were now part of a dynamic living organism. There was new life in worship. People actually wanted to pray together. Nearly every present member and every new Christian was willing for prayer for the release of the power of the Holy Spirit. We genuinely wanted to "do" the Word not just hear it, although as with holiness, these things do not happen overnight. Obviously there were many imperfections, but we could talk about them, repent and pray together. Commitment to one another and the leadership deepened. There was a sense of acting as one. We did not want to act in dangerous isolation. We were most definitely not "clones" and there is plenty of discussion. But sharing became something we wanted to do, particularly in prayer over matters affecting the church. In fact, this has become one of the outstanding features of our church, so that we have reached the point where nearly everything to do with the church and its wider mission is conceived, born and bred in corporate prayer. People were glad to seek God about their gifts and ministries and for those to be affirmed in a corporate context.

Above all we gradually became outward looking. It took about three years after the first Service of Dedication, but now the church hums with evangelism. The sense of urgency to win the world is what makes us tick. On average at present about fifty people are won to the Lord each year, in what is a hard materialistic area, and there is a *net* increase of approximately twenty adults per year to our weekly area groups. From the original one hundred and twenty-nine who took part in the Service in 1983, seven years on there were nearly two hundred and fifty in the adult ministry groups. This may not appear to be wildly "successful" but each one of those people is aiming towards the Vision and is a functioning member of the Body. We realised with awe and gratitude that there actually was a living Body in Hawkwell, the Body of Jesus himself, worshipping in spirit and truth, encouraging one another and reaching out with the love of Christ to those outside. It is imperfect, yes. Every now and then there is a skin infection or a broken toe or whatever. But by and large we are well and glad to be alive in these days, for his glory.

We were also very practical about facilitating the diversity arising from the unity. Gradually the vast majority of the work of ministry of the church was being done through the re-structured home groups. They are weekly housegroups with a difference. Each has its own "patch" of the parish, and the emphasis is on being outward-looking. So although there is the usual fellowship and teaching, there is also intercession, and housegroup evenings regularly designated for planning for or doing evangelism. Most members have a different role – host, teacher, intercessor, pastor, evangelist, administrator, social organiser. These people facilitate those particular activities by the members. The pastor, for example, would ensure that not only is each member cared for, but that pastoral visits are carried out in their "patch". In this way true delegation became a reality, so that the staff were able to act in the role of "conductors of the orchestra", drawing out the different talents. Old and young, men and women, single and married – all were included. There is also a "general" midweek group for Bible study and prayer for those who did not want to be involved in "ministry", but who want to attend a weekly fellowship group. We have planted congregations within the parish, so that our regular attendance including young people, enquirers, new Christians etc., as well as housegroup members, totals nearly five hundred. Sadly, there is no church building in the parish which is big enough for us all to get together occasionally.

The church as an "army"

As we became this living organism so we were able to discover what it means to be an *army*, that third concept of the Church in the New Testament, which has come to mean so much to us. We are learning what it means to "stand firm in one spirit, contending as one man for the faith of the Gospel without being frightened in any way by those who oppose" (Philippians 1:27,28). Obviously to some extent the experience of being a building, a body and an army have overlapped. This is especially the case when stressing unity, which is equally important for an army as for a body. No church should engage in "spiritual warfare" unless there is a fair degree of unity, or the enemy will make mincemeat of us.

It is certainly the military picture of the Church which God is stressing to us at the moment as we have entered into what may by God's grace prove to be a third seven-year period. Many Christians are puzzled when, after the sense of wonder, joy and peace which overwhelms them when they first trust in Christ, things seem to go wrong and problems arise which perhaps are unlike anything they have experienced before. It could be that no one has warned them that Christians are "at war". Before we come to Christ the enemy concentrates his efforts on keeping us out of the kingdom of light. He may even see to it in some cases that life seems good and that some are surrounded by material comforts – anything to lull people into a false sense of security. But once an individual is transferred from the kingdom of darkness to the kingdom of light, then a new strategy is needed. The enemy now majors on seeking to render

Christians ineffective in God's Kingdom. This is fairly common knowledge to most believers, although it is amazing even so that we either forget the devices of the evil one and so are unprepared, or we give in to them.

The majority of Christians may gradually learn how to deal with temptation or oppression, but are totally unaware of the significance of the local church in God's Kingdom, and therefore that the enemy will direct much of his attack against the local body of believers. It is quite obvious from any reading of the book of Acts and the epistles, that the isolated Christian was the exception rather than the rule, and that was only in extreme circumstances such as imprisonment. The whole impression is of the importance of the Church, the corporate body of Christians. Immediately after Pentecost "All the believers were together . . . every day they continued to meet together" (Acts 2:44,46). They were "one in heart and mind" (Acts 4:32). After Stephen's death severe persecution forced most believers to move out of Jerusalem (Acts 8:1). They preached the Word and new churches were formed in each town. God had his strategy. I am convinced that Jesus intended the known world of the time to be evangelised, after the initial missionary work of individual believers, by his Body in each place. The enemy therefore devised his tactics. At first he concentrated on persecution of individual believers. They were mobbed, flogged, imprisoned, tortured, martyred.

Gradually we notice a change in the enemy's strategy. He begins to attack the churches. We see from the epistles that there was chaos in the church at Corinth (1 Corinthians), and later, when that was sorted out by

Paul's impassioned plea for order without quenching the Spirit, there was a reaction against his authority (2 Corinthians). In Galatia there was a serious threat to the Gospel by Judaisers, people who sought to reintroduce legalism. In Thessalonica some were downing tools to wait idly for the Second Coming (1 Thessalonians 5). Paul had to warn the Ephesian elders to guard the flock against heretics and divisive people (Acts 20:17–38). It seems from Revelation 2:2 that his words were heeded.

However, generally speaking, by the time we reach the book of Revelation, which is thought by most scholars to have been written c. AD 95, later than the epistles, we are into a different scene. St John was exiled on Patmos off the coast of Asia Minor. He wrote to the seven churches nearest to him. The enemy had been at work in serious ways, and the message from the Lord Jesus to all but two of the churches included a severe warning about the need for repentance, followed in some cases by a conditional prediction of judgement. An interesting point is that in each case John writes to the *angel* of the church in Ephesus or Smyrna, etc. If this is taken literally it is an indication that the victory would only be won in heavenly places. In any case in the teaching of St Paul in Ephesians 6:10–18 we are warned that although we might appear to be dealing with human opposition, all the time "our struggle is not against flesh and blood, but against the rulers, against the authorities, against the powers of this dark world, and against the spiritual forces of evil in the heavenly realms." The book of Revelation goes on to lift the curtain to give us a glimpse of the mighty battle being fought between demonic and angelic forces. Recent popular Christian novels have once more made believers aware of these unseen forces, although they fall into the trap of depicting evil as obviously ugly, when so often the devil is clothed as an angel of light.

One can see different enemy tactics used against the Church throughout history. Persecution and heresy are the two most common, although the devil never appears to learn that the former only serves to purify and strengthen the Church. Then one can see division (Orthodox and Catholic, followed by much sub-division after the Reformation), and institutionalism. Intermingling of Church and state, power politics, worldly church leaders can all be recognised as enemy tactics. Sins in the Church became even more blatant prior to the Reformation – immoral popes; indulgences purchased, supposedly to buy salvation; total ignorance of the Bible even by priests, because of the insistence on the use of Latin – all these glaring faults and many more besides are well known. We have of course already looked at the enemy's strategy in the present, majoring on deception leading to apostasy.

The enemy is totally ruthless in his determination to exterminate the Church, or at least render it ineffective. He knows that it is the major plank in the visible restoration of God's rule. He attacks ecumenical movements, denominations, Christian leaders especially of national or international standing, and of course, local churches. The devil chooses to forget the Cross until reminded of it by believers. He has convinced himself that he will still win. After rebelling against God before human history (Isaiah 14:12–15), he was permitted limited domain over planet earth (Job 1:6–12, Matthew 4:8–9, 1 John 5:19). His defeat was ensured by the death and resurrection of the sinless God-man (Colossians 2:15), but he fights on, refusing to accept defeat. It is only by faith in God's word that we know he will ultimately be *shown* to be utterly defeated (Revelation 20:7–10).

Until that time, there is a war on! Every Christian is involved whether he likes it or not, whether he is prepared or not. How much better to be aware of the battle and to know how to use the weapons provided by God. I believe that although no true Christian can be deprived of eternal life, yet any believer who does not know how to fight will be ineffective. He will certainly not be an "overcomer" (Revelation 12:10–11).

I am also convinced that any local church, of any denomination or none, throughout the world, which does not learn to engage in spiritual warfare in these Last Days, will either disappear without trace, leaving only scattered believers, or will become apostate.

We need to understand that the enemy, in addition to his overall campaign of vitriolic hatred towards the people of God, is likely to have a particular strategy against each church. Although we must not waste time fearfully looking around to discover this, for it is far more important to teach positive truth, yet when things go wrong we need to remember the teaching of Ephesians 6. We have found that although it is very difficult and probably unhealthy to try to anticipate the enemy's next move, yet if we keep alert we can nip it in the bud in the early stages.

We were almost totally ignorant of such things in our early years in Hawkwell. We were told about the witches' covens in the woods nearby, but failed to recognise the serious attack in our midst for what it was.

I have mentioned the extreme tendency to division which, as Tony and I came to understand more about the principles of building the church, was focused especially on the two of us in the form of bitter criticism. It was quite out of proportion humanly speaking to any issue involved. I was accused by three different people of being demonised. It took about six years for it to dawn on us that such opposition was a major strategy of the enemy – in fact there was probably a principality of rebellion over the church.

In one sense this sort of thing can never be "proved". It can only be discerned by the leadership of the Body by faith on the basis of the glimpses given in Scripture. We prayed about it for some time until one Good Friday four leaders believed the Holy Spirit was showing us that this was God's time for us to "bind the strong man". We did so in prayer, using scriptural language and promises. To our amazement, the atmosphere in the church very quickly changed, so that there was an openness for the positive teaching on unity described earlier. There were just a few "mopping up" operations after that, mainly connected with a handful of "ready made" leaders from other churches who thought God was calling them to Hawkwell. We were slow to discern that they had not in their hearts grasped our corporate Vision, but were still living back in the very different days of personal renewal of the sixties and seventies. This problem of seemingly "mature" Christians moving to a new church, in some cases wanting power without commitment, is encountered by many churches. We blame ourselves for too readily inviting such folk into our own leadership, for what was usually to prove a short-lived period. Virtually the final fling of the principality of rebellion was when desire for power seized a key leader who sought to divide the church against us. He has since apologised for this. In fact many years later there has been reconciliation with a number of people who figured in our early traumas. One man wrote to apologise that he used to lead a group praying against us. A lady approached us at a Renewal Conference to say that she viewed things very differently now. Some who went to worship at nearby churches and refused even to speak to us are now happy to relate to us socially. The teenage or grown-up children of others came back to worship in our church.

Although the war goes on, we were thankful that the war zone moved from inside our church although different battles were to follow later. I would like to say that it is now entirely out in the world, in connection with evangelism. However, we soon discovered that there were also battles connected with the wider Church, some of which have been described. This will obviously be on-going, especially in connection with interfaith and New Age infiltration.

After three or four years of relative peace and positive development in our own church, we were to discover that we should have taken more notice of Paul's warning to the Ephesian elders for constant vigilance over the flock. The enemy tried a number of new devices. One was to send along a confidence trickster. This was my first experience of such a person infiltrating Christian circles. He spoke so convincingly of his spiritual pilgrimage, that if it had not been for the gift of discernment followed by prayer, which led to discoveries as to his true nature, we could have been taken in. In fact he was involved in a double life, and once he realised we knew, launched a vitriolic campaign against the church. The congregation had to be warned; with the bishop's knowledge he was not permitted to be confirmed to receive Holy Communion, and eventually there was specific prayer for his removal which "worked" after a testing time of a few months.

We more recently saw the enemy trying a more subtle tactic of tempting folk to opt out of leading roles here, by causing other avenues of service to appear more attractive. Whereas it is right for some to be sent out by the church, and this has happened, and I hope will in the future, in other cases it is deception with folk likely to end up with far fewer opportunities to spread the Gospel than are possible from here, with our national and international contacts. Although this could appear to be simply human error, there was the same sense of oppression as in previous attacks. Symptoms included apparent temporary personality changes which could also affect those dealing with the situation, inability any longer to hear and feel the heartbeat of the Body here, or to want any corporate prayer about the matter even though it affected the church, and a feeling of waves of darkness seeking to batter at our defences. It happened in two cases but once recognised, was brought to a happier resolution in a third, so we are trusting that is the end of that tactic, after a time of fasting and prayer. Praise God that even where a situation is not resolved positively with the people concerned, he can through prayer and by his victorious power turn any situation to his advantage.

We have noticed different strategies in connection with other churches. The enemy might seek to infiltrate a church with immorality, or legalism, or ensure it is dominated by past history, sometimes going back decades or even centuries. As the devil is very inventive, it is important for the leadership of a church under attack to ask God for wisdom about the particular strategy directed against them. After that it is important to know what to do about it. The Old Testament stories of battles are so helpful here. Joshua, for example, had to ask God about the particular divine plan for attacking each fortified city. The Jericho method was only right for that particular town. God had something different for Ai, which Joshua discovered rather belatedly (Joshua 7 and 8). So it may be that a church's leadership might discern that one or more of the following methods of battling (to name just some) are required: lengthy prayer and fasting; repentance about a particular aspect of church life; exorcism of buildings; praise walks or marches; personal approach to an individual; closing down an organisation or activity; deliberately clothing oneself with the opposite spirit (e.g. generosity where there has been stinginess or materialism). Sometimes, as in our case, there comes a specific moment when the demonic force can be declared to be bound.

We have just discovered from a newly converted ex-Satanist that there is concerted nationwide prayer against key renewal ministries, including the ministry based in Hawkwell. It is good when God causes the enemy to reveal his hand, because it is a back-handed form of encouragement that one is involved in a ministry he considers worth particular attention. Such discoveries should not cause us to be fearful, but rather we should remind ourselves that "the one who is in you is greater than the one who is in the world" (1 John 4:4). Actually he is infinitely greater – Jesus fills the whole universe (Ephesians 4:10). The enemy is only a created being; powerful, yes, but as nothing compared with our Creator God.

But how can our personal struggles or our local church battles with the enemy have anything to do with the worldwide panorama which is unfolding before our very eyes, as the End Time events begin to unfold? It is as we overcome in each situation, ensuring that we operate as a Body, that God's Kingdom is extended and the power of darkness pushed back. Yet although as a church we are still learning how to be an army, how to battle and overcome, we are looking forward to becoming, with all God's people, more like a fourth picture of the Church: the Bride of Christ.

CHAPTER NINE

The Way Ahead

On one occasion when I was praying, in my mind's eye I "saw" the British Isles as if from a satellite. A red glow was beginning to appear over the arc of the horizon nearest to Britain, but the surface of the land was pockmarked with craters, like the surface of the moon. The interpretation which I believe was given to me in prayer, was that in his mercy it is on the heart of God to want to send revival (the red glow) to rescue as many as possible from the enemy. But the craters sadly represented many places which claim to be churches, and purport to be centres of worship, but are in fact places of danger where those rushing for safety could stumble and fall. The impression I had as I prayed was that although there are obviously churches which are alive, the overall picture was one of danger. Our church had once been more of a crater than a place of safety, but that was changing, and that transformation could happen to many more.

Reaching out to the wider Church

So it was that a longing was born in my heart to serve the wider Church, around the time when God gave a specific commission to the Body in Hawkwell, to fulfil Acts 1:8 – "You will receive power when the Holy

Spirit comes on you;. and you will be my witnesses in Jerusalem, and in all Judea and Samaria, and to the ends of the earth.''

There was a time when we were so taken up with the problems of our own parish that we were scarcely able to take any notice of anything beyond, let alone do anything about it. But now God was telling us not only to evangelise our neighbourhood, but to look beyond to our county, our country, even the ends of the earth. We knew this would mean going, not just writing out cheques. We came to realise too that the commission was not so much to engage in direct evangelism beyond our parish, but to share with other churches the scriptural principles God has taught us. In that way we dared to believe that dozens, if not hundreds, of other ''local'' churches would be turned inside out. They too would become dynamic living organisms, the Body of Christ, and having dealt with the enemy within, would be able to engage in intercession, spiritual warfare and evangelism, in order to fulfil Acts 1:8 themselves. Perhaps Britain could be covered with at least as many beacons of light as craters, so that if God were to send revival it would not be dissipated. Obviously ''churches'' where a false Gospel or no Gospel is preached are the biggest craters. But churches which are divided, or which seek to please men rather than God, or do not challenge to commitment, or are inward-looking, are unlikely to be much help to unbelievers or new Christians.

So the ABWON Link Church Ministry was born and developed rapidly under that name during the years 1986–90. Tony majored on the other side of ABWON: the prophetic witness to the Church of England. I spent most of my time on the interdenominational Link Church Ministry, although there was mutual sharing and support, under Tony's spiritual oversight. As a couple, however, we were only the spearhead of a work which involved the whole Body of our church (and more recently of other churches) in prayer, practical work, giving and going. As a church we are small in number by world standards. We are just a bunch of ordinary people. But since we took the first faltering steps to obey Acts 1:8, we have seen God do extraordinary things through us. Surely that is Jesus' purpose for every church?

Although there are a number of church growth ministries, most of which have a great deal to offer, we believe the Link Ministry was unique in a number of respects. Firstly, it was run by a local church, teaching only those biblical principles which we are seeking to implement, if imperfectly, ourselves. Secondly, it could not become a big "empire" because it operated on the "strawberry plant" system: namely, if a Link Church became ready for the wider implications of Acts 1:8 that church in turn reached out to other churches. The Link was only for a couple of years or so, except where Ministers asked to be used in extending the principles to others. Thirdly, each church which requested it was prayed for during the two-year period by another Link Church. Fourthly, we found the principles to be effective in churches of any denomination or none in a number of countries. Churches could be rural, town, suburban, inner-city; small or large; struggling or thriving but needing further direction. Lastly, we gave practical help about getting over the pain barriers before a church becomes "one in heart and mind".

Vision was combined with method, prayer and power with practicalities. Not one Link Church was a Hawkwell clone, I am happy to say, for churches are as diverse as people. In five years we formed ninety Links in England, four in Wales, one in Scotland, two in Northern Ireland with many more interested since a recent visit, and one in the Republic of Ireland. There are over forty in New Zealand, and one each in the USA, Holland and Sweden, which are countries we have not yet visited, and one in Rome. After three years' working with churches in New Zealand the Link Ministry was indigenised, as would be our policy in each country. We visited New Zealand three times and went on to Australia. We shall soon be visiting South Africa and look forward to ministry there.

We suffer and rejoice together as churches battle in some cases through very traumatic situations. It is apparent, however, that the worst of the internal battle seems to be over far more quickly than it was with our church. Nevertheless, the warfare can be intense. This can be understood by considering that only the rule of God can push back the rule of Satan. If he hates this in the life of an individual, how much more is the wrath of the enemy aroused when a local church seeks to come under the lordship of Christ? Demonic forces which have perhaps been established in a church or neighbourhood for years, begin to thrash about in fear of being pushed out. Praise God for his victory!

Apart from half a dozen churches which made a false start, we give God the glory that all the Links gained at least some benefit, e.g. deepening prayer life or more outward-looking home groups. Some were already full of life and outward-looking. It was not so much quantitative but qualitative growth which was required, particularly deeper unity, or a sense of direction. Perhaps fifty per cent of the Link churches would look back to the formation of the Link as a major turning point, and perhaps twenty-five per cent have been totally transformed under God. Usually there was some contraction, or at least concentration on the inner life of the church, before expansion. We have not been going long enough to point to dramatic results in evangelism, particularly as we largely work in countries where evangelism is very hard. Nevertheless, there is sufficient evidence of God's people being turned inside out, being given a heart for the lost, a longing to be true disciples of Christ and a desire to reach out to the wider Church.

At the beginning of 1991 Tony and I, with the backing of our church, relaunched our wider outreach ministry for the Decade of Evangelism. We have renamed it *Time Ministries International*. (ABWON is just retained for Tony's mailing list.) We chose the world TIME because it has a prophetic note of urgency, as well as standing for "Together for Intercession, Ministry and Evangelism". We want to reach as many churches as possible with our principles and resources, without the strings of a Link, unless ministers choose to have a prayer link. We have described it as "a prophetic ministry which stresses the place of the local church of any denomination in the purposes of God. Unity on a biblical basis is encouraged within each church, for the purpose of intercession, every member ministry and evangelism in the power of the Spirit. Emphasis is placed on every Christian being called to serve as a member of the Body of Christ. First leaders, then members are invited to study a course leading to a service of dedication. Ministry groups are then formed to carry out the work of the church and to witness to the love of Jesus Christ.''

What better method for the decade of evangelism than to envision entire local churches for outreach? This is what we long to do, in the belief that it is God's plan "A" for evangelism, but also in the knowledge that because the battle is so fierce, each evangelising church needs to be a united army as well as a functioning Body.

Our desire as a local church is that in this small way we might be used to help prepare the Bride for the return of the Bridegroom. This is another metaphor for the Church which has become important to us. Jesus does not want to come for a Bride dressed in tatty clothes, or one who is half-hearted, or even worse, easily seduced by others. In my imagination I sometimes wonder if one of the last temptations of Jesus was of the devil showing him glimpses of the Church in the future, perhaps riddled with formalism or materialism or liberalism. Worst of all, that luke-warm Church which Jesus wanted to spew from his mouth. Perhaps Jesus countered that temptation with the picture later to be given in Revelation 21 of a bride beautifully dressed for her husband. God has had his "trophies of grace" down through the centuries, of individual believers and churches, and I believe this trend will continue to be the case, even though the world grows darker.

A worldwide network of churches

But what of the glaring disunity in the wider Body? How will the Bride be made ready in that respect? First, a look at the present scene. We have all witnessed attempts at ecumenical unity which usually result in more division than before – the new "united church" and the two strands on either side which want to remain as they were. We also must avoid the new trap of the one-world religion – the multifaith mishmash which will come. What about unity in the renewal scene? At first it seemed that all those who were beginning to experience a greater release of the power of the Spirit were being drawn together across denominational barriers. Then renewal began to focus once more on denominations, as people realised that structures of churches needed to be transformed in order to progress beyond renewal of the individual. But often the resistance of the hierarchy was found to be so great that people gave up hope, and the focus unfortunately reverted to emphasis on the individual, with an over-emphasis on inner healing and counselling. Yes, people still come together for celebrations, to find what is lacking in their local church, but there is much disillusionment about the possibility of transformation of churches within historic denominations. Yet we and others have proved that transformation of such a church can happen by God's grace and power, if only the church leadership is prepared to be of no reputation and follow Jesus' plans to build his Church. In some cases, where this did not take place, church members joined the newer "housechurches" in the UK. There were accusations of sheepstealing, not without some foundation, but mainly it was a case of sheep wandering off to find greener grass. That phase is largely over, and housechurches have either fossilised or become outward-looking in evangelism. Some have resisted any wider structuring, but others are definitely new denominations. Other Christians remain in their original church to intercede for transformation.

Charismatic leaders seek to meet together but the general picture is still one of disunity. Personally, I do not think God could trust us with a totally united worldwide Church. Who could possibly be entrusted with its leadership, and could unity ever be achieved without serious compromise? Would it not be better just to work towards good relationships, recognising creativity in diversity, whilst excluding outright heresy?

In New Testament times there was perhaps just one group of believers in a small town, or a number of groups meeting in homes, usually "underground" during a time of persecution. One imagines that perhaps they tried to get together if at all possible, or at least the leaders did. Paul was able to write "To all in Rome who are loved by God and called to be saints" (Romans 1:7), knowing that his letter would at least be passed round or copied out to be read to the majority of believers.

Many Christians picture something similar in the future – a loose-knit network of churches in relationship. The need for good relationships will become increasingly important, especially if most of the hierarchies of the major historic denominations become apostate, taking many with them, as New Age/Interfaith/One World unity movements gather momentum. Only those local churches which are seeking to apply biblical principles in the power of the Spirit will survive deception (although individual Christians will escape), and they will increasingly need each other.

The apostate church could join the persecutors, and those true to our Lord may have to "go underground". Those who have remained lone but faithful witnesses, or as a keen but tiny group, within increasingly liberal churches, will need to join at this point those churches which remain more true to Scripture. In a city or larger town there could be a number of such churches, in a village perhaps only one. This kind of scenario is probably the case in China now, and has been in other countries which have known persecution. Some faithful believers have remained in the State-controlled churches, but that would need to be a specific call from God, especially in the future.

It is vital that no one seeks to pre-empt God's timing for this to happen worldwide. Their efforts would only result in some other denomination or even sect being formed. Attempts to form the "pure church" humanly have always ended in this way throughout church history. In Time Ministries International we stress that radical transformation is possible at a local church level within any denomination as it is now, given faith and obedience. That is what we shall continue to stress unless there is a major new turn of events. That would have to be something really disastrous, such as the uniqueness of Jesus as the only Saviour being officially denied. However, one practical step that can be taken now to assist the formation of a network of biblical churches, is that when clergy and other ministers are moving to a new church, they do not move to one near to an already existing "live" church of another denomination. What on earth is the point of farming the same ground, when there are vast tracts left without a biblical witness?

God will no doubt raise up a leadership in the future at least over towns or areas for the persecuted and more purified church. But any who actively *seek* to be *world* Christian leaders or prophets will be by-passed, because God will not give his glory to another. He is not interested in the power-hungry. He will have his own means in his own time of raising up leadership. He will no doubt use "the weak things of the world to shame the strong. He chose the lowly things of this world and the despised things – and the things that are not – to nullify the things that are, so that no one may boast before him" (1 Corinthians 1:27–29). I would stress again that the ideal could be for area leaders to be in fellowship, as opposed to the monolithic hierarchical nature of the apostate churches. The New Agers are into networking, and usually the enemy copies and counterfeits what he sees as God's plan. In our ministry we saw the importance of a network of biblically-based churches, two or three years before we heard of the use of the term in the New Age. Obviously Time Ministries International is only a tiny part of God's plan to form a worldwide network of churches, of any denomination or none, which resist apostasy and, even better, are prepared to be radically transformed to operate in unity and power especially in evangelism. It may be in the near or far-distant future that the parting of the ways from what will be the apostate church takes place. Even then, Christians should resist the creation of new denominations. Meanwhile we work within existing structures.

The "true" Church worldwide may eventually have to learn to live without its cathedrals and other fine buildings; its hierarchical structures; financial resources; its pomp and show. Those things could all be in the hands of the nominal church. There may even be no access ultimately to the media, videos, tapes or literature. We in the West are so rich in these things, but poor in spirit compared with perhaps our brothers and sisters in China and elsewhere. We shall in times of persecution need to revert to the simplicity of New Testament days, and in so doing, rediscover more of the power of the Spirit. There will then be only spiritual buildings. We shall have to function as the Body of Christ in each place. We will of necessity need to be companies and battalions in God's army fighting not just for survival, but rather learning how to invade the gates of hell. Far better to learn those principles now, than to have to start from scratch then.

The revelation of God's sovereignty

If a Christian is forcibly isolated, then God will give grace in that situation as we know from numerous testimonies. But normally he would intend to establish his rule over families, over local churches, and over the loose network of churches which remain true to his word. Even then, the Church will not be completely pure – that will not happen until Jesus returns. Meanwhile he will be working out his plans for nations and for creation. Christians should of course always be working for God's will in society and against injustice and oppression. We should be working, too, for conservation in nature (and any view of being in the End Times should never be allowed to militate against that). But God has a greater plan. If the millennium means anything, it surely means the coming of that time eagerly awaited by creation, when the sons of God will be revealed. I am not referring to any strange "Manifest Sons" theology, but simply the teaching of Romans 8:18. How important that the kingdoms of the world and creation itself one day see just how powerful God's work has been in his Church, despite the worst that Satan could throw against it. I believe that both those who are unduly pessimistic about the future of the Church, and those who are over-triumphalist, are mistaken. Rather, as with so much profound truth, we are faced with paradox. There will be deception, persecution, desertion and tribulation. There will at the same time be discernment, triumph, perseverance and glory.

How vital too that God should demonstrate his rule over nations (from Jerusalem – Zechariah 14) and over the old order of creation (Isaiah 65:25). It is inconceivable that Jesus should not be seen to be Lord over his world and his creation before the final show-down with Satan. Only then will we see the destruction of the old world and the creation of the new heavens and earth (2 Peter 3:10,13; Revelation 20:7–21:5), which I believe will be as real and as similar to the old, as will be our new bodies compared with out mortal bodies. It will be as Jesus' risen body was, compared with his earthly body. There is no biblical justification for a view of a spooky heaven inhabited by ghostly creatures.

All this may be far off, it may be near. It will certainly transcend not only my own cursory and tentative thoughts about the meaning of Scriptural prophecy, but those of all Christians put together. We shall no doubt all be rebuked for being foolish and slow to believe *all* that the prophets have spoken. But the central feature in God's plan to establish his Kingdom will be the revelation to the world – to all human, angelic and demonic powers – of God's masterpiece, the Church. This glorious Bride, formed as a result of the death, resurrection and ascension of Jesus, indwelt by the Spirit and beloved of the Father, will be presented to his Son for all to see. "Now to him, who is able to do immeasurably more than all we ask or imagine, according to his power that is at work within us, to him be glory *in the church* and in Christ Jesus, throughout all generations, for ever and ever" (Ephesians 3:20,21).

Satan's attacks on Christians and leaders

When one glimpses something of the magnitude of God's plan it is all the more obvious that Satan will attempt to ruin it, and all the more a cause of grief when Christians and churches give in to his wiles. Christian leaders are a particular target, as one after another falls to immorality, pride, deception or is simply sidetracked from being in the centre of God's will.

Tony and I find ourselves constantly in a position of encouraging men and women at the level of local church leadership to be single-minded, to make themselves of no reputation, to fear God rather than man. So many clergy and pastors try to keep everyone happy, but end up pleasing no one. Others allow themselves to be dictated to by the whims of a power-hungry minority. The church suffers and so does the minister. Far better to suffer for following the will of God and for leading a church courageously in his way.

As we have moved in circles of wider Christian leadership, we see in others the sort of struggles we now face. Having laid down reputation perhaps in the home church or denomination, there is the subtle temptation of gaining repute with a different grouping. There is the constant problem, despite all efforts to prevent it, of people putting church leaders on a pedestal. Even if this does not lead to pride, it can lead to unwanted distance between oneself and members of the Body. For purely practical reasons one is no longer able to be involved in the healthy nitty-gritty of everyday church life. Then there is the unpleasant surprise of discovering envy and rivalry between Christian leaders in different ministries, who actually have much in common.

Tony and I are always more conscious of failings in ourselves than in others. That is partly why we need the support and correction of the local Body. We have the privilege of having a prayer group in our church who pray especially for Tony and me. The leader telephones us every week to discover our particular needs and prayer requests. We are so thankful to God for their love and perseverance. The whole church in fact supports us in prayer. Church members everywhere should be more aware of the need to pray for their leaders. The greater reward in heaven will probably go to the faithful unknown intercessor, rather than to the Christian leader jetting around the world, speaking to crowds.

God's purpose of holiness

Perhaps the greatest leveller for us all is when we consider the matter of personal holiness. Who among us would dare claim to be holy, in the sense of sanctified (as opposed to the sense which applies to all believers, of being set apart for God)? I am convinced that the heart of holiness is to know the truth of Galatians 2:20: "I have been crucified with Christ, and I no longer live, but Christ lives in me." As self-denial in its true sense can appear a negative thing, conjuring up pictures of monks lying on beds of nails, many are anxious to display the positive side, of channelling self-sacrifice into good works for others. It is much harder if one's God-given calling is not so obviously connected with relieving the needs of one's fellow men. But God sees our motives, as his word "judges the thoughts and attitudes of the heart" (Hebrews 4:12). A person involved in good works might be engaged in them for the satisfaction of praise of men or because it makes him feel useful. Someone else with a more hidden ministry might be fulfilling it more out of love for Jesus and people.

Holiness may seem elusive, but I found very illuminating a comment quoted long ago to James Hudson Taylor by his friend John McCarthy. "The Lord Jesus received is holiness begun; the Lord Jesus cherished is holiness advancing; the Lord Jesus *counted* upon as never absent would be holiness complete." In the end it is all by faith: "In the same way, *count* yourselves dead to sin but alive to God in Christ Jesus" (Romans 6:11).

If the revival we long for does not result in a greater measure of such holiness amongst the people of God, then it will be no revival. That is why I believe the enemy will try to hi-jack even the holiness/revival movement, so that people flock after a star-studded cast rather than Jesus himself. I am at present struggling with what may be a prophetic insight which has come to me recently, of the awful possibility of even a counterfeit or at least mixed "revival" taking place. Experiences we had at charismatic conferences in 1990 confirmed our suspicion that large sections of the renewal movement are moving away from Scripture. We grieve deeply at this as we are convinced that the Holy Spirit inspired much of the Renewal which swept the Christian world since the 1960s. If revival soon seems to be sweeping the Church through the influence of these groupings which are straying from Scripture, what does that say about the "revival"? But rather than distancing ourselves, I believe God could be saying that Christians who are renewed, *and in practice still hold to the supremacy of Scripture above experience*, should stay involved in order to bring biblical insight to bear. In that way, out of the seeming chaos of an impure revival, God could still bring about true holiness-centred revival. The judgement, about which I have written earlier, could be the pain of being involved in this whole process, and of seeing even some "renewed" sections of the Church becoming apostate. Whether this is so or not, I believe we are near to the last chance for the Church to experience true holiness-centred revival, leading to a rescue mission type of revival out in the world which can only be the sovereign act of God.

Two kings and two prophets

When I was last in Jerusalem the ancient story of two kings and two prophets was impressed on my mind in a way which shed light on a possible final revival. I was staying in Christ Church Guest House just inside the Jaffa Gate. It is immediately opposite the Citadel, which dates back to Crusader times but has Herodian foundations. It has recently been opened as a museum, which provides fascinating insight into the history of Jerusalem.

I was particularly interested to discover more about the time of Hezekiah's reign, as I happened to be reading about that in my prayer and Bible study times. We also saw in the Jewish quarter of the Old City part of the wall which was built in his day. Those were difficult days to say the least. The Northern Kingdom of Israel had been defeated by the Assyrians, and Samaria captured. Hezekiah was King of Judah in the South. Before him the evil King Ahaz had strayed so far from God's ways, that he had even offered up children in sacrifice to false gods. Hezekiah carried out many far-reaching reforms, but it seemed that the only reward he received was more trouble. "After all that Hezekiah had so faithfully done, Sennacherib, king of Assyria, came and invaded Judah" (2 Chronicles 32:1). The whole account of what happens is recorded three times in the Old Testament: 2 Kings 18–20, 2 Chronicles 29–32 and Isaiah 36–39. It is also well attested by archaeology. The ruthless war-machine headed by Sennacherib brought about the capture of no less than forty-six cities of Judah. One can see in the British Museum the actual reliefs dating from 701 BC depicting these conquests. In his annals Sennacherib tells of the 200,146 people taken captive, and how he made Hezekiah "a prisoner in Jerusalem his royal residence, like a bird in a cage". But he does not say he took Jerusalem. In fact, at this point God intervened in a miraculous way. Hezekiah prayed, Isaiah prophesied, and a terrible calamity overtook the mighty Assyrian army. Shortly afterwards, Sennacherib was murdered by his son. Jerusalem's future was secured for a century to come.

Many Christians would like to think that we are at a similar stage in Western history. Judah had experienced a chequered career from the time of the division of the Kingdom into Israel in the north and Judah in the south. The history in 2 Chronicles in particular shows that a "good" king who obeyed God was usually followed by one who "did evil in the sight of God". Ahaz, who preceded Hezekiah, was one of the worst. Yet after allowing limited punishment, God had mercy when there was renewal, repentance and reformation under Hezekiah. Many people believe God will do the same today.

Yet on that same visit to Jerusalem I saw the gate dedicated to Huldah, which reminded me of a similar account of another king and prophet. But this story has a different ending. Josiah, who reigned nearly a century after Hezekiah, was a reforming king as well, seeking to put right the evil of his predecessors, Manasseh and Amon. We read in 2 Kings and 2 Chronicles of the impact made on the life of the young Josiah, when the Book of the Law of the Lord was found during renovation work on the temple. The people renewed their covenant with God and this was followed by a total reformation, which included demolition of detestable idols as well as restoration of good practices, including the Passover. Yet all this was carried out in the full knowledge that God, through the mouth of his prophetess Huldah, had only granted a short reprieve, for disaster would surely come to Jerusalem (2 Kings 22–25; 2 Chronicles 34–36). Approximately twenty years after Josiah's death, Jerusalem, the holy city of

God, and the glorious temple of Solomon, lay in ruins.

Why? Why was it that Isaiah was able to prophesy: "I will defend this city and save it, for my sake and for the sake of David my servant"? Yet a century later Huldah was only permitted by God to tell Josiah that although *he* would not see it, "the Lord says, 'I am going to bring disaster on this place and its people.' " The answer can only be that in the mystery of God's wisdom there comes a time when he says: "You've gone too far. Enough is enough."

The last revival?

I believe we are at that stage in Britain, in the West and Westernised nations. Yes, there could be revival, if the people of God give themselves to repentance, weeping, prayer, and pleading for holiness. It will be a revival born out of judgement on the Church, as with grief in our hearts we witness increasing apostasy. It will be a revival which in itself brings the judgement of purification, including the pain of separation from the apostate church. Christian leaders in particular will come under the searchlight of God, as he looks up and down our nations to see those who will follow him wholeheartedly. He looks for those who will speak out against idolatry, compromise and watering-down of his Word. He looks for those who will lead the flock entrusted to them along the difficult way, the way of the Cross. He is not interested in obviously "successful" churches, however full and however seemingly good the worship. He is not even interested in how many healings or deliverances take place, or even how many "professions of faith" there may be. "Not everyone

205

who says to me, 'Lord, Lord,' will enter the kingdom of heaven, but only he who does the will of my Father who is in heaven. Many will say to me on that day, 'Lord, Lord, did we not prophesy in your name, and in your name drive out demons and perform many miracles?' Then I will tell them plainly, 'I never knew you. Away from me, you evildoers!' '' (Matthew 7:21–23). Those hard words are immediately followed by what we often regard as a children's story of the wise man who built his house on the rock. It actually has an adult message – for to stand on the rock is to hear the words of Jesus *and* put them into practice (v. 26).

That is what God is interested in. He is looking for leaders who will do that themselves, and challenge church members to be true disciples, who demonstrate their faith by living a life of true discipleship. Far too many clergy and pastors go for the lowest common denominator, or over-emphasise signs and wonders to produce church growth. Jesus never did that. He set his face to go to Jerusalem to die, and he expected his disciples to follow. Only church growth and miracles which flow from sacrifice count in God's sight.

Tears came to my eyes when I read in an *Open Doors* magazine the true story of a girl, who, in 1988, at the age of seventeen, became burdened for the lost in a province of China near Tibet. Her church believed that she had a true call from God, so they sent her with a female companion to go on a mission to Qinghai. The climate was inhospitable, they were often hungry. After six months of fruitless wandering they heard a child sing a Christian song. They discovered a believer and soon there was a small church of fifteen people. But cultural differences were great and evangelism was tough. They toiled and were homesick. Only one letter from home reached them after eighteen months, to indicate there might be other Christians coming to help. So they saved their meagre food to share with the reinforcements. But nobody came. Telling her story at a secret evangelists' conference in China in 1990, everybody began to weep with the young woman. Though disappointed, she was determined to go back to Qinghai to continue in evangelism. Surely God will honour her dedication, for it is out of such sacrifice that revival is born.

How poor we are by comparison. There are so many Christian workers, so many ministries, so many resources, so much money. We enjoy freedom, conferences, glorious worship led by gifted musicians. We even see signs and wonders. But where is the sacrifice?

If we allow God to change our hearts, if we plead with him to show us how to die to self, then the Church will see true revival. But it could be the last opportunity to make an impact on our countries. It will certainly be the *only* way to make that impact.

God has allowed his NOW time for our Western nations. It will not be long before the night comes when no one can work. The revival as it reaches beyond the Church will be a rescue mission to save as many as possible from the darkness which threatens to engulf us. The West has chosen the New Age religion. For example, in West Germany, just before its union with East Germany, there were according to *The Theological Revue*, thirty thousand clergy, but ninety thousand registered witches and fortune tellers. (And even as I write this book I am learning that is is a race against time to ensure that is not the dominant influence in

Eastern Europe and possibly even Russia.) That does not mean that the enemy has won. He is a defeated foe even though he deceives himself to believe otherwise. But it does mean that God is permitting the judgement of our own choice to come upon our nations.

The crossroads

Those who claim to be Christians, believing in the Bible as the inspired word of God, need to wake up, whether we call ourselves evangelicals, charismatics or prefer some other label or none. We are at a crossroads. The broad road, which can be entered by compromising the truth of God's word, looks so tempting. We could easily get caught up in its traffic only to find that we are travelling along with New Agers, interfaith enthusiasts, prophets and miracle workers who appear to be Christians but are demonised, as well as those of another religion or none. It is a road of bright lights and fast-moving traffic. It is the way of tolerance – to be at one with everyone, at one with nature, at one with our world.

By contrast the way ahead may seem to hold little attraction. It is only for those who, as a result of true faith in Jesus and by the power of his Holy Spirit, seek to follow his Word. It is the way of revelation not imagination. The way is too dangerous for the isolated individual. There are many tempting New Age diversions or side roads to compromise. We need to band together in small, disciplined companies. We need to learn to listen to our Commanding Officer's instructions. We need to consult our Guidebook regularly. We need to be united as companies and relate to the rest of the army, so that we are able to ward off attacks, and withstand the persecution meted out to those who proclaim Jesus as the *only* Saviour. There is an urgency about the whole operation. This is no selfish escape route. One of our main tasks is to make as many sorties as possible to rescue people from the dangers of the broad road which leads to destruction. Many will only respond when they are nearly run over, or find themselves in a pile-up. For many, experience of redemptive judgement will be the only means through which they are prepared to call on the rescue services. Although it seems impossibly humanly, those who travel on the narrow road will be characterised by joy. And there will be the glory of countless thousands being rescued from the kingdom of darkness.

I understand only a little at present as to how this scenario for the Church in Westernised nations relates to the bigger scene worldwide. There is rapid expansion of Christianity in China, and other areas in the Far East, parts of Africa, South America and elsewhere. There are millions as yet unreached with the Gospel, and an enormous population explosion in third world countries. Praise God that there are something like eighty major plans to win the world for Christ by the year 2000. We trust that many of these are in the centre of his purposes. Over a third of them involve over one billion dollars. But eventually Christians the world over will face the same testing time as is over-taking the West.

As the enemy seeks to further his plans to gain total control of the earth, which is his goal, it is possible that he will appear to change tactics as his cover is blown. So many Christians are exposing the New Age in America, and at last in this country, that Satan may see to it that the actual term becomes passé. It could be that something in the nature of a One World Movement takes over. But the basic strategy of "transforming" human consciousness so that man calls upon supposed divine powers within, will remain the same.

Whether we live in the West which is turning its back on Jesus, or in a country where people are responding eagerly to him, the enemy will sooner or later try out this strategy. But the glorious truth is that the Gospel message remains the same and has its age-old power to transform lives. God had planned his strategy before time began. It will never be popular, because the Cross is at the centre. It was never meant to be a shining, attractive ornament. The Cross was ugly; the Son of God died there in agony, separated in an "eternal moment" from his Father. It was all because of sin. The true Gospel message will always proclaim these facts first, with a call for deep repentance and commitment in faith to the One who died in our place. So many preachers gloss over this so that they can speak of benefits to be received. Sometimes it seems they are more eager to offer physical healing than spiritual. This may appear to have "worked" in its appeal, but now the enemy is in competition, offering apparently similar benefits. Of course, there are genuine blessings, and miracles, because God loves to give good gifts to his children. It is also more possible to experience sheer enjoyment of life than ever before when we belong to him.

Yet there should really be only one true motive for proclaiming or responding to the Gospel message. God is God. There is only One. He is Love. He is the

Creator. He alone is worthy of worship and total allegiance. But man is estranged from him, not primarily because of sins committed but because of the sin of rebellion against God. There is only one way back: God's Son. "I am the way, the truth and the life. No one comes to the Father except through me" (John 14:6). The only divine power available to human beings lies not within ourselves, but as the Holy Spirit, the third person of the Trinity, invades our very being as we respond to God through Jesus by faith. That is the only way to eternal life with God. Those who do not respond have withheld allegiance from God the Father, preferring self or another god. This can only bring eternal separation from the Creator.

It is important to stress that the heart of this message is not judgement but love. Satan, whatever his pretence to the contrary, basically hates all human beings. But God is Love. True love, which sees and knows all, yet still loves to the point of death. That is why the Gospel message has such power. The whole power of God to transform any man, woman or child, from the most upright citizen to the worst sinner or most demon-possessed. New Agers can be and are being rescued. It is never too late in this life for those who have compromised even the uniqueness of Jesus Christ, to repent. Ultimately all the wiles of the enemy will come to nothing and Satan himself will be destroyed. The last enemy to be destroyed is death. "Then the end will come, when [Christ] hands over the Kingdom to God the Father after he has destroyed all dominion, authority and power" (1 Corinthians 15:24).

Meanwhile, the ideal response of each believer is perhaps best summed up in Psalm 138.

I will praise you, O Lord, with all my heart;
before the "gods" I will sing your praise.
I will bow down towards your holy temple
and will praise your name
for your love and faithfulness,
for you have exalted above all things
your name and your word.
When I called, you answered me;
you made me bold and stout-hearted.
May all the kings of the earth praise you, O Lord,
when they hear the words of your mouth.
May they sing of the ways of the Lord,
for the glory of the Lord is great.
Though the Lord is on high, he looks upon the lowly,
but the proud he knows from afar.
Though I walk in the midst of trouble,
you preserve my life;
you stretch out your hand against the anger of my
    foes,
with your right hand you save me.
The Lord will fulfil his purpose for me;
Your love, O Lord, endures for ever . . .